THE
WORSHIP
PLOT

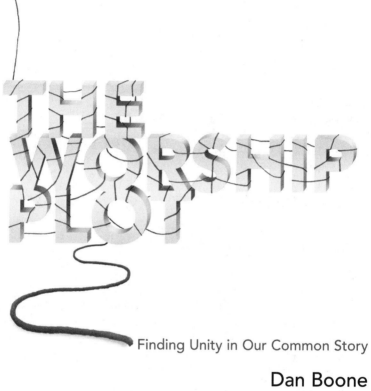

Finding Unity in Our Common Story

Dan Boone

BEACON HILL PRESS

OF KANSAS CITY

ISBN-13: 978-0-8341-2312-0
ISBN-10: 0-8341-2312-6

Printed in the United States of America

Cover Design: J.R. Caines
Interior Design: Sharon Page

Library of Congress Cataloging-in-Publication Data

Boone, Dan, 1952-
    The worship plot : finding unity in our common story / Dan Boone.
       p. cm.
    ISBN-13: 978-0-8341-2312-0 (pbk.)
    ISBN-10: 0-8341-2312-6 (pbk.)
  1. Public worship. I. Title.

    BV15.B66 2007
    264—dc22

                                                          2006103316

10 9 8 7 6 5 4 3 2 1

CONTENTS

PREFACE

My concerns are many. It concerns me when a pastor adds drums and drama, thinking he or she has gone contemporary. It concerns me when people argue over stylistic changes to worship without ever engaging significant theological questions. It concerns me when worship leaders import megachurch worship models without running them through the grid of their own history and theology. It concerns me that the future generation of worship leaders (now sitting in classes, chapels, and congregations) has no strategy for unifying a diverse people in worship. It concerns me that undue congregational energy is spent on in-house worship change to the detriment of outbound compassion, justice, and mercy. It concerns me when brothers and sisters retreat to the worship bunker of personal preference and begin to lob grenades at the opposing bunker. It concerns me that the one event meant to celebrate our unity—common worship—is the event that fractures and splinters us. So, you can see, I have my concerns.

But I also have high hopes. The worship that occurs in most sanctuaries is great worship—not because we are brilliant—but because the people come to do the work of worship. And this work did not begin with an order of worship. It began in the heart of God, who is the self-emptying love known as Trinity. True worship is the fellowship of the Father who sends the Son who gives the Spirit. And even as this shared life flows to us, it flows back as the Spirit empowers the sacrifice of the Son on our behalf, as a pleasing response to the Father. Trinitarian theology guides our understanding of worship. We are not creating something new but rather stepping into a stream that began in God.

I have written at a lay level, because I believe worship belongs to the laity, the people of God. Worship is about their offering in Christ through the Spirit to the Father—not about a platform performance. It is my hope that this book will find its way to the battlefront where worship wars are currently being waged. I hope to lower the octane of the discussion and increase the meaning of the conversation. I offer this book as a gift to communities that care about worship. Too many churches have been wounded by friendly fire. Maybe I can spare you a few wounds.

My highest hope is to encourage you and your people in your journey of lifelong worship.

—Dan Boone
January 2007

INTRODUCTION

Plot: noun. a chart or diagram; a secret plan to accomplish some questionable purpose; the scheme or pattern of the events, incidents, or situations of a story or play.

verb. to make a plan; to plan for secretly; in math, to draw a curve through a series of points to go from A to B to C.

—*Funk and Wagnall's Standard Desk Dictionary*

We're familiar with these definitions of *plot*. We know about assassination plots, property plots, and character plots. We've seen plots unfold in murder mysteries and connect-the-dots coloring books.

But is worship plotted? Do subversive people scheme weekly behind closed doors? Does worship move sequentially like a John Grisham novel? Should worshipers be connecting the dots from A to B to C, from song to sermon to prayer? Is there an outcome toward which we are moving?

Or do we believe that worship is an unplotted event? That the Spirit mysteriously takes our random choices and organizes them on the fly? I grew up thinking that bulletin-plotted worship orders actually deprived the Holy Spirit of room to work. A good worship service had no preaching and featured altar traffic and surprise testimonies—things I still find very meaningful.

I love spontaneous moments in response to the Spirit of God. But I also think it is important for us to listen to the story of our creative God. In the beginning, the Spirit hovered over a dark, formless chaos. Then God went to work. The result was order, structure, and story. The order did not confine God; it unleashed God. The structure did not inhibit God; it revealed God. The story did not limit God; it narrated God.

In worship, the creating Spirit of God is at work sustaining the life of a people. The structure of worship is conducive to life in the Spirit. The story of God and humans is being told and acted out, much like a play combines words and actions to produce compelling drama.

Even as I write, a worship war is going on somewhere in a church. Some of these wars are simmering. Some are sizzling. Pulpit or no pulpit? Drums or organ? Guitars—maybe, if we don't plug them in. High liturgy, low liturgy, no liturgy? Preaching in formal or casual attire? Hymns or choruses? And if choruses, how many repetitions? If hymns, can anybody explain "terrestrial balls" and "sacred throngs"? Use of movie clips or ban Hollywood from the sanctuary? Plainspoken words or PowerPoint sermons that seem to scream, "Pay no attention to that person behind the pulpit!"

The division of the Body of Christ over worship style is a sad chapter in the story of a grand people. While our story is about the Spirit who makes us one, our worship wars make us winners and losers—mostly losers.

Could it be that we will never find unity in style but

that we can find unity in plot? What if, week after week, we celebrated and dramatized the same plot, the same story?

In this book I suggest five acts for the drama of worship.

1. **Entrance.** A play starts with an exposition that sets the time and place of the story. The Entrance does something similar for worship. The opening act of the worship plot locates us. We gather at a certain time— on Sundays—because God has called us together. We enter a certain space—God's presence. Gathering reminds us who we are and whose we are. This Sabbath pattern is our distinguishing habit.

2. **The Bad News.** Just as a first act in a play raises a conflict that intensifies during the second, so goes the unfolding of the worship plot. If it really sinks in that we are gathered in the presence of the Holy God, we instantly identify with Isaiah: "I am ruined! For I am a man of unclean lips, and I live among a people of unclean lips, and my eyes have seen the King, the LORD Almighty" (Isa. 6:5, NIV). That's another way of saying, "What's a person like me doing in a place like this?" This leads to Act II of our drama, confession of the Bad News, the admission that our lives aren't all we hoped they would be, or all that God has desired for us.

3. **The Good News.** This is the climax of our drama, the turning point for the better—the Good News. The

Bible is full of good news. "I have heard your cry." "And the father ran out to meet him." "Get up. Take your mat. Go home" (see Exod. 3; Luke 15; Matt. 9). Every one of these statements is made to people living with bad news. Good news can exist only in the context of bad news. The Good News can be delivered as scripture, sermon, or song. It is the moment in the service when we declare to troubled people that God is with us doing something redemptive. It is the story of Father, Son, and Spirit acting in loving aggressiveness toward troubled humans. We grow numb under worship that drones on and on about sin in a dark world. The worship plot must get from Bad News to Good News, from sin to grace, from death to life.

4. **Response of the People.** The Good News opens us and makes us capable of response. Like the falling action in the fourth act of a play, our response to the Good News should draw us to an outcome where we are better off than we were before. The Good News even suggests what our response might be. The possibilities are many: repent of sin, be baptized, sing a song, give money, volunteer to serve, dedicate an infant, share the Lord's Supper, testify, offer words of encouragement to fellow worshipers, be silent, break bread. These are real, bodily responses to the Good News. We believe that hearing is not enough; we must do something.

5. **Blessing.** Another word for *blessing* is *benediction,* which means "to say good words." This act of the worship plot takes only a minute or two, but it is the needed conclusion. It's the denouement of the drama, where we hear that we are better off than we were. A pastor lifts his or her hands and pronounces blessing on the people who have gathered in God's presence, been honest about their Bad News, received the Good News, and responded to grace. These people are now ready to be sent into the world where Jesus has already gone. They will serve the people of the world, empowered by the grace they have received. This closing blessing is a gift. It gives boldness to the beaten-down. It whispers grace to the weak. It invades our damaged self-esteem with words that say God values us. The grace of the Lord Jesus, the love of God, and the communion of the Holy Spirit go with us all.

Style divides. Story makes us one. I've seen the story (Entrance, Bad News, Good News, Response of the People, Blessing) lived out in all kinds of settings: camp meetings in Sartinsville, Mississippi; a church of three in New Salem, where Aunt Tiny missed more notes than she hit; splendid sanctuaries with robed choirs and rattle-your-bones pipe organs; down-home Southern gospel gatherings, and contemporary services using every imaginable creative art.

I've concluded that if we look for our unity in the common story we share, maybe we will learn to worship together.

THE
FIVE
ACTS

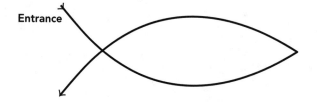

Entrance

ACT I
Entrance: Locating Ourselves

I knew I had been away from home too long. I was on a five-week jaunt with several preaching assignments in several locations. This morning I woke up in a strange room and couldn't remember where I was. The fog lifts slowly for me in the mornings. Add a couple of time zones, a different pillow, strange surroundings, and I've got a fog that almost won't lift. It took a few minutes before I could locate myself.

Knowing where we are is a major part of knowing what we are supposed to do. When I figured out where I was—a bed and breakfast in Marion, Ohio—I had a clue about my day.

The Entrance is Act I of the worship plot, the first in a series of connect-the-dots that leads us into the Story of God. Some label this act the call to worship; others, the invocation. Like the exposition of a play, the Entrance locates us in time and space.

The entrance of a home, a building, or a room usually tells you where you are. A locater—a street sign, an address number, or a room number—is normally nearby. People who are looking for a place want to be assured they are there when they arrive. I looked past one of those entrance locators one time and wound up in a women's restroom. Thankfully, it was vacant. We need locators at the Entrance of worship that tell us where we are. Some of the locators are already in place.

Location in Time

God's people are located in time by observing the Sabbath. After six days of labor, we wake up on day seven and refuse to go to work. Only slaves work seven days a week. We know from the Exodus story that our slave days in the Goshen brick-making factory are over. God liberated us. As free children of God, we've been told to keep the Sabbath. Every seven days we locate ourselves in time by resting. Long before God spoke about a sacred place, He spoke of a sacred time. "And on the seventh day God finished the work that he had done, and he rested on the seventh day from all the work that he had done" (Gen. 2:2). And He called the day holy. God sanctified time by giving us the Sabbath.

In Christian tradition, we observe the Sabbath on Sunday, the first day of the week. This is the day of resurrection, the day God begins making all things new. We begin each new block of time by gathering to worship the God who liberates us from slavery and raises us from the dead. Sabbath is our entrance into the new week. By gathering in our sanctuaries, we recall who we are in time. We are the free people of God, filled by the renewing Spirit, gathered for worship, sent into the world as Jesus is sent into the world.

Location in Space

The God who locates us in time also locates us in space. Abraham came to realize the value of holy places. He piled stones in a heap to mark the spot where God spoke to him. As God's family grew, God gave Moses instructions for a tabernacle. A holy place was sanctified in the middle of the camp. When God's family grew larger still and settled in towns and cities, a temple followed. The Spirit-engine of the Temple was the holy of holies, the innermost shrine of the life-giving Spirit. The arrangement of the Temple from outer court to inner shrine was designed to remind people of their location in the presence of a holy God.

The idea of a holy place fell into disarray when people began thinking they could consign God to a location. They tried to keep God in a sanctuary, go visit Him on Sabbath, then leave Him behind as they went out to live. But God refuses to stay in His room. God is always moving out into the world and refuses to be managed or kept by His creatures. Stephen, in the speech that led to his martyrdom, declared that God will not live in temples "made with human hands" (Acts 7:48). Stephen was suggesting that God's preferred temple is a community of people.

The architecture of our buildings can be a wonderful reminder to us that we are God's people. But beautiful architecture alone can never contain God. As we enter the Sunday morning sanctuary, we need to remember we are a called-together people. God resides in the middle of the gathered Church, not in the building. A place is made sacred when God lives among the people gathered there.

In April 2000, I was in Moscow working with Christian leaders. We toured several cathedrals in the Kremlin. As I entered these beautiful churches, my eyes were instantly drawn to the vivid color of the icons that adorned the insides. The story of Jesus surrounded me in color, art, and beauty. The Orthodox Church, much better than we Protestants, understands the need to engage our senses in the worship of God. I was sensually engaged in worship as I "read" the story of Christ in icon after icon. It was a moving experience. As I stood in each cathedral, I felt located. I knew where I was. I was standing in the story of Jesus.

A day later, I worshiped at a Protestant church in Moscow. Fifty to 60 believers gathered on the upper floor of a rented building. The local grocery store was their next-door neighbor in the three-store strip mall. Folding chairs were set up. Portable instruments were brought in. Pulpit furniture was set in place. And we began to worship. One woman testified to the transformation that had come into her life. She graciously thanked a missionary for coming to her city. He then walked all the way to the back of the sanctuary where she stood. He embraced her. The beauty of Christ in that moment rivaled any icon I saw. God does not live in temples made with hands. He lives in His people. But these people do gather in temples made by hands.

How rich it is when our facilities are God-honoring in both ways—reminding us of our story in the beauty of the surroundings and filled with people who are the temple of God's Spirit.

Centered in Time and Space

We exist in time (Sabbath) and space (sanctuary) because God has called us. God draws us together in time and space so our lives may be centered.

- Without a center, life is fragmented.
- We don't know who or whose we are.
- We become slaves of technology who spend all our time at work.
- We become slaves of pleasure who spend all our time at play.
- We become slaves of boredom who spend all our

time with mind-numbing television programs and computer games.

- Without God as our center, we are scattered in every direction without meaning or identity.
- We don't know where we are.
- Morning fog becomes life fog.
- We live in anxiety and fear.
- Our life has no boundaries.
- We chase advertisements, seductions, and pagan pied pipers.
- We manipulate and are manipulated.
- We stuff our souls with numbing placebos.
- We are caught up in the latest diet fad, the newest car, the fastest computer, the trendiest restaurant, the hottest movie.
- Our life has no center. We are dislocated.

But imagine a patterned life of gathering once every seven days in a familiar setting with the people of God. Imagine a lifetime of being reminded who you are. Imagine a lifetime of centering and recentering your life in Christ.

The Entrance is the act in the worship drama that does this. Can you see and hear it now?

"Good morning. This is Sunday, the Sabbath gift of God to us. We are free children of God. We are gathered in God's presence today because God—the same God who gives us work to do Monday through Saturday—this God has called us here. We are not in the workplace, so we can forget about producing and selling. We are not in front of a television, so we can forget about being entertained. We are not in a classroom or lecture hall, so we can cease our mastery of knowledge. We are in the presence of the God who longs and loves to set us free. God is up to something good in our lives this morning. It is good that we are here."

We open our hymnals and begin to sing,

Praise to the Lord, the Almighty, the King of creation!
O my soul, praise Him, for He is thy health and salvation!
All ye who hear,
Now to His temple draw near;
Join me in glad adoration!

Praise to the Lord, who o'er all things so wondrously reigneth,
Shelters thee under His wings, yea, so gently sustaineth!
Hast thou not seen
How thy desires all have been
Granted in what He ordaineth?

—Joachim Neander

What are we doing? We are locating ourselves in the presence of God. We are entering His presence together.

We may go on and sing "Holy, Holy, Holy! Lord God Almighty" or invite people to "Worship the King." We may follow the lead of those who have gone ahead of us in worship and read psalms together:

Make a joyful noise to the LORD,
    all the earth.
  Worship the LORD with gladness;
  come into his presence with singing.
Know that the LORD is God.
    It is he that made us, and we are his;
    we are his people, and the sheep
        of his pasture.
Enter his gates with thanksgiving,
    and his courts with praise.
  Give thanks to him, bless his name.
For the LORD is good;
    his steadfast love endures
        forever,
    and his faithfulness to all
        generations *(Ps. 100)*.

The Entrance of the service can last 5 to 10 minutes. It can include a prayer of invocation, music, silence, scripture, a welcome. It can begin with a worship video combining scripture, nature scenes, and music.

It can have variety. A child can walk onto a bare platform and tell people that God enjoys the playful worship of His people. A person from another nation can remind the congregation that worship is a privilege. Other possibilities will come to mind as we think creatively about the opening moments of worship. These various elements are stitched together to tell us we are in the presence of God.

As we look over the five acts of the worship plot, we will find that Acts II and III, the Bad News and the Good News, will suggest how we will shape Act I. For instance, if the Good News is "God can be counted on to keep His word," and the Bad News is "we live in a world of broken promises and lies," then the Entrance could locate us in the presence of the God whose words are faithful and true. The worship leader might begin the service like this:

"Good morning. Do you know anyone who has never lied, never fudged, never shaded the truth? If anyone comes to mind, you've probably seen God or one of God's children. This reliable God has called us together this morning. We are in the presence of One who hates shadows where lies lurk and duplicity prowls. God is a straight shooter. What God says today may be hard to hear, but we can know it is true. Let's open our hearts to the God who sees it and tells it like it is."

Then we sing "Come, Thou Almighty King": "Come, and Thy people bless, / And give Thy word success . . ." (anonymous, ca. 1757); or "My Faith Has Found a Resting Place": "My heart is leaning on the Word— / The written Word of God . . ." (Lidie H. Edmunds).

We next read Ps. 19 and are reminded that God has spoken truthfully in creation and in holy law. A prayer of thanks is offered to the God whose words are dependable. This sets us up to move into the Bad News—that we live in a world of broken promises and lies.

Perhaps the Good News is "God is no respecter of persons" (Acts 10:34, KJV) but offers grace freely to every creature. The Bad News is "we live in a world of prejudice and favoritism." The Entrance on this Sunday might be like this:

"Good morning. Have you ever thought that God has it out for you? That others are higher on God's help list? Do you consider yourself low on God's totem pole? Well, for those who think this, I have good news. God loves all of you, especially those who think they are on the least likely list. We are in the presence of a God who offers grace to every creature. Let's stand and sing together."

And your voice joins with others as you sing,

> *There's a wideness in God's mercy,*
> *Like the wideness of the sea;*
> *There's a kindness in His justice,*
> *Which is more than liberty.*
>
> *There is welcome for the sinner,*
> *And more graces for the good.*
> *There is mercy with the Savior;*
> *There is healing in His blood.*
>
> *For the love of God is broader*
> *Than the measure of man's mind;*
> *And the heart of the Eternal*
> *Is most wonderfully kind.*

If our love were but more simple,
     We would take Him at His word;
And our lives would be illumined
     By the presence of our Lord.
                                        —Frederick W. Faber

Then we read from Ps. 103, where we learn these things:

- God knows what we are made of.
- God has a Fatherlike compassion on His children.
- God's steadfast love lasts forever.

Next, a child tells the congregation that her mother sometimes asks her if she knows how much she is loved. With arms stretched as wide as possible, the child answers, "This much." Isn't it good to be gathered in the presence of a God who loves us "this much"? But then, not everyone in our world experiences such love—and you are into the Bad News.

In shaping the Entrance, you center on the action and character of God that will be declared later in the Good News. A sermon on truth telling calls for an Entrance highlighting the God whose words are dependable. A sermon on favoritism calls for an Entrance emphasizing the God whose arms are stretched wide in love. This means the preacher must work far enough in advance to suggest Entrance themes to the musicians and service planners. Otherwise, people will sit down to a Sunday morning potluck mystery soup.

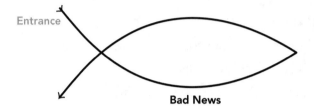

Entrance

Bad News

ACT II
The Bad News

As I write this, I am in San Diego for a conference, staying in room 1522 of the Wyndham Emerald Green Plaza Hotel. This place has all the bells and whistles, with a price tag of $181.63 a night. It goes against my southern Mississippi roots to lay out this kind of cash for a hotel room. I've paid less for a car. Simplicity feels a lot better in my soul than fancy hotels. My family thinks I'm ex-travagance-challenged. Being here causes me to look in the mirror and ask, "What's a guy like me doing in a place like this?"

Likewise, we sit down in the church sanctuary and are located by Act I, the Entrance. We find ourselves in the presence of a holy God, a sovereign God. This God knows us through and through. In His presence, we tend to look at ourselves and ask, "What's a person like me do-ing in a place like this?"

I think Isaiah thought that. The angels located him

with their singing: "Holy, holy, holy is the LORD Almighty" (Isa. 6:3, NIV). As soon as he realized where he was, Isaiah cried out, "I am ruined! For I am a man of unclean lips, and I live among a people of unclean lips, and my eyes have seen the King" (v. 5, NIV). "Ruined"—that was Isaiah's word for it. Not a bad word. I call this the Bad News.

Between this holy God and people like us there is a gap. On our best Sundays, we still have sin sitting in the pews. Into the presence of this holy God we bring our

- Grasping anxiety
- Mouthy words about others
- Attitudes toward authority
- Marital frustrations and fissures
- Prejudice
- Tendency to nitpick people raw
- Festering wounds
- Misuse of power
- Bodily abuse
- Selfish posturing
- Lies of overestimation and flattery
- Secret dark places
- Preoccupation with image
- Love of money

These things don't stick out in the world's shadowy lands, but put them under the blazing searchlight of God's holiness and they stick out like a Volkswagen on a Mercedes lot. This is why it must be made clear in the

Entrance, the first act of our drama, that we have gathered in the presence of God.

And if our personal hearts are clean and clear before God, then our corporate hearts still need to confess. None of us has graduated from praying the Lord's Prayer: "Forgive us [corporately and personally] our debts, as we also have forgiven our debtors" (Matt. 6:12). In Isaiah's words, "I live among a people of unclean lips" (Isa. 6:5).

In America, babies are aborted, the gap between the haves and the have-nots is widening, the church is segregated, greed runs rampant, the environment is soiled, and entertainment is dehumanizing. I could go on. Each country has its own collection of destructive behaviors.

When we confess our country's sinful behaviors, a watching world will know how deeply we feel about the destruction of God's creatures and creation. We live as servants of Jesus in a sinful culture. The road dust of this world clings to our feet. We are not untouched by the evil around us. If we view ourselves as Christian escape artists who slither through the Monday-to-Saturday world, unfazed by its seduction and influence, we are only fooling ourselves. We must name the influences, behaviors, and powers that run a dark world. We must confess before God that we need cleansing.

Beyond all this, there is a brokenness among us that must be brought before God. We have been hurt, lied to, taken advantage of, manipulated, raped, stabbed in the back, neglected, divorced, robbed. What shall we do with this stuff? The world offers no place to take it. The church invites people to bring it with them to corporate worship and confess the brokenness to God.

By labeling this act of worship Bad News, we are saying it is healthy to admit what is wrong in front of God. Like the rising action in a play, the Bad News intensifies for us how far we are from God's holiness. Act I, the Entrance, has located us in His presence, and now we see things with increasing clarity. We can say right out loud that our lives aren't what we'd hoped they'd be. Or even more, what God wants them to be. We can admit that our society is on a downward moral slide. We can declare that we hurt deep inside. We can utter our sickness and grief, our failure and sin. We can admit what is bad about the world we live in. This second act of worship is what separates the publican from the sinner.

Two men went up to the temple to pray, one a Pharisee and the other a tax collector. The Pharisee, standing by himself, was praying thus, "God, I thank you that I am not like other people: thieves, rogues, adulterers, or even like this tax collector. I fast twice a week; I give a tenth of all my income." But the tax collector, standing far off, would not even look up to heaven, but was beating his breast and saying, "God, be merciful to me, a sinner!" I tell you, this man went down to his home justified rather than the other; for all who exalt themselves will be humbled, but all who humble themselves will be exalted *(Luke 18:10-14)*.

It's true the two lifestyles are different. But Jesus was calling attention to something else. The Pharisee approached God by spotlighting the difference between himself and the tax collector. The Pharisee recognized the superiority of his morality. And he was right. His ethics were higher. His morals were better. Given the choice between the Pharisee and the tax collector, we'd much prefer to have the Pharisee as our roommate, next-door neighbor, or employee. Yet the Pharisee registered disapproval in God's eyes. And the tax collector went home justified? Why? Simple. The Pharisee measured the gap between himself and the tax collector and thought himself righteous. The tax collector measured the gap between himself and God and saw his sin. Paying attention to the distance between us and God is a vital act of worship. God honors humility and confession. God resists pride and posturing.

If we are among those who believe God can enable us to live a holy life and avoid intentional sin, we sometimes struggle with confession. Our optimism about the radical nature of transforming grace makes it hard for us to be publicly honest about our sin. Some of us feel we're slipping into a casual acceptance of sin if we confess weekly. So rather than confess weekly, we confess weakly. But I would suggest that people being made holy may have the best vantage point for confession. As our hearts are filled with love for God and humans, we are given God's eyes to see the destructiveness of sin in us and around us. As one dear saint confessed, "The closer I get to the holy God, the more my own shadows are exposed."

The Bad News act of the drama of worship is a vital prelude to hearing the Good News. God comes to people who are broken. God appears in the middle of bad news. Jesus frequented bad-news scenes:

- The tomb of a friend
- The side of an adulterous woman about to be stoned
- The table where sinners gathered
- The unclean turf of a leper
- The home of despised Zacchaeus
- The bedside of a sick child
- The Road to Emmaus with two hopeless travelers

The Bad News is the opening through which God comes into our life. When we gather and admit our Bad News, we are opened for the coming of God. Confession is the soul unlocked, opened for exploration by the divine Helper.

Everything I've written so far about the Bad News might lead you to think this is something we must do for ourselves, something necessary for our peace of mind—like a good housecleaning or a soul catharsis. But to think this way would be disastrous. It misses the main part of Christian worship. To simply show up and think our role is to confess our sins and receive forgiveness is to rob Christian worship of its central character—Jesus.

When it comes to the Bad News, Jesus has taken our sin upon himself. Jesus stands as our High Priest offering the only acceptable sacrifice for our sin. Jesus represents us to God. Apart from Jesus,

- We cannot confess.
- We cannot pray.
- We cannot offer ourselves to God.
- We have no mediator.
- We have no one who leads us to the throne of grace and the seat of mercy.
- We have no one who has died in our place and named our sin.
- We cannot worship.

Jesus stands in our place, before God, admitting our sin. Jesus is praying for us. Jesus is offering himself as our sacrifice.

> Consequently he is able for all time to save those who approach God through him, since he always lives to make intercession for them. For it was fitting that we should have such a high priest, holy, blameless, undefiled, separated from sinners, and exalted above the heavens. Unlike the other high priests, he has no need to offer sacrifices day after day, first for his own sins, and then for those of the people; this he did once for all when he offered himself. For the law appoints as high priests those who are subject to weakness, but the word of oath, which came later

than the law, appoints a Son who has been made perfect forever *(Heb. 7:25-28).*

Since, then, we have a great high priest who has passed through the heavens, Jesus, the Son of God, let us hold fast to our confession. For we do not have a high priest who is unable to sympathize with our weaknesses, but we have one who in every respect has been tested as we are, yet without sin. Let us therefore approach the throne of grace with boldness, so that we may receive mercy and find grace to help in time of need *(4:14-16).*

As you plan this second act of the worship plot, be deeply conscious that the Christ who stands praying for us has already revealed the Bad News. He is the Spirit at the heart of our confession to God. This empties us of any wrongheaded thought that reconciliation to God was our idea or initiative. It begins and ends with Jesus.

Making the Bad News Move

Act II, the Bad News, can take many shapes. For years it existed in the form of prayer requests. People named out loud what needed divine attention, from the sick to the jobless to the lost. In many ways, this was one of the best things we did. It reminded us that worship happens in a needy world. It interrupted the clean flow of an antiseptic service that avoided our real pain. It served as a raw reminder to those who like "seamless" worship, that our world cannot be orchestrated without dead spots and untimely interruptions. We even gave place to "unspoken requests." We knew there were things so bad they couldn't be mentioned out loud. But when someone raised a hand or said, "I have an unspoken request," we knew there was pain in the house. Bad news had come to the sanctuary that day. Worship meant something.

In many churches, the prayer request ritual has been exchanged for something else. We probably tired of the recital of everyone's sick list. In larger churches, this could take too long. Instead of the public naming of bad news, some churches have an open altar during the congregational prayer. The songs that invite us to come pray inform what we are doing:

> *All your anxiety, all your care,*
> *Bring to the mercy seat—leave it there.*
> *Never a burden He cannot bear,*
> *Never a friend like Jesus!*
> —Edward Henry Joy

> *Are you weary, are you heavy-hearted?*
> *Tell it to Jesus; tell it to Jesus.*
> *Are you grieving over joys departed?*
> *Tell it to Jesus alone.*
> —Jeremiah E. Rankin

Many of the hymns we sing are prayers. These can be read together as petitions. Try praying these hymns: "I

Need Thee Every Hour," "Open My Eyes, That I May See," and "Spirit of God, Descend upon My Heart."

In liturgical traditions, prayers of confession became a standard part of worship. The *Book of Common Prayer* offers this:

> Most merciful God,
> we confess that we have sinned against you
> in thought, word, and deed,
> by what we have done,
> and by what we have left undone.
> We have not loved you with our whole heart;
> we have not loved our neighbors as ourselves.
> We are truly sorry and we humbly repent.
> For the sake of your Son Jesus Christ,
> have mercy on us and forgive us;
> that we may delight in your will,
> and walk in your ways,
> to the glory of your Name. Amen.*

In other services, the worship leader simply says, "Let us confess our sins to God." A time of silent prayer follows.

Getting at the Bad News

Confessional prayer is one way to make the Bad News move, but there are many other possibilities. Drama is a

---

Book of Common Prayer (New York: Church Hymnal Corp, 1979), 320.

strong possibility. In a drama, it is possible to act out the
Bad News. We see humans in front of us behaving badly.
They make wrong choices, say the wrong things, and
weave webs of sin. If the drama is done well, we are
drawn into it. We identify with characters. We laugh or cry
at ourselves. A drama resembles a parable by pulling us into a certain way of looking at things. I find that open-end-
ed dramas have the best effect. If everything is resolved in
the drama, there is little left for the preacher to do with the
Good News text. A drama opens us to the reality of Bad
News and prepares us to hear the Good News.

Another way to get at the Bad News is an interview.
In a service that dealt with the story of the Gerasene demoniac (Luke 8), we invited the local chief of police to tell
us about the wildness in our community. Another time,
in a service built around the commandment "Thou shalt
not kill" (Exod. 20:13, KJV), we invited the mother of a
murdered child to talk to us. It is hard for most churchgo-
ers to feel the weight of this commandment. We normally
end up talking about killing each other with words and
looks. But after hearing the interview with this mother,
we were open to the Good News of the commandment.

In many churches the Bad News often creates a clash
of values. We once used a clip from a movie that was
well known in our culture and had spawned several
phrases and values. The clip we selected contained no of-
fensive words or scenes. It simply depicted a corporate

executive defending the habit of greed. This executive made a moving, mesmerizing speech suggesting that greed is good. The audience in the movie gave him a standing ovation. That video clip was the second act of the service, the Bad News. It followed an Entrance that had drawn our attention to the generosity of God's love. The plot line of the worship was

Entrance: God is generous.

Bad News: The world believes greed is good.

Good News: The radical grace of God moves us from greed to generosity.

Our people were brought face-to-face with the issue of greed in their economic world. Because we brought the world's finest argument into the sanctuary via video and challenged it with a radically different perspective, they were confronted with the difference. The kingdom of God invaded the kingdom of darkness. Pre-Christians called us honest, relevant, and willing to deal with things that mattered. The prevenient grace of God was at work in their hearts, opening them to being saved.

But the response of several long-term believers could not have been more different. Anonymous cards said things like, "I suppose the staff watches movies all week to find this material"; "I have to see this type of thing all week long. I come to church to get away from it"; or "Doesn't it send a mixed message when we say, 'Be discerning in your entertainment choices,' but still show clips from evil movies?" Each of these is a legitimate question. We came back the following week and answered each one. To the first question, "No, our staff doesn't sit around watching movies all week. We use a resource book, published by a Christian company, suggesting movie clips and contemporary songs on given themes." To the second question, "We all live in a world of greed. We all tire of it. But the church is not an escape hatch or an enclave for saints. It is a gathering of people at the invitation of a holy God. We do not gather to escape the world, but to be cleansed of the world, filled with the Spirit, and sent into the world with an alternative option." And to the third question, "Yes, this could be construed as sending a mixed message. But over the long haul, we are consistent in challenging our people to make entertainment choices that refresh the soul, reflect God's heart, and restore us to vibrant life."

Prayer, confessional texts, drama, video clips—these are not the only ways to get at the Bad News.

- Send a person to the mall with a video camera and a question:

    What do you hate?

    What makes you worry?

    What's the hardest thing about marriage?

    What do you think about sin?

    Assemble the answers into a person-on-the-street video.

- Open the local newspaper and read an article about something that happened in your community.
- Project the words of a pop song, or play it. Allow it to become the voice of darkness that invades our cars, homes, and offices. Rather than letting it stand outside the sanctuary unchallenged, bring it before God for consideration.

The issues around contemporary expressions of the Bad News are volatile. The pastor has to be grounded in theological reality. Jesus stands in this act of worship revealing something deeply wrong. This is not about entertainment, shock value, or being contemporary. It is about naming our sin as Jesus has revealed it. Pastors who do these things for shock value are dangerous.

Many congregations are not geared to handle a contemporary expression of the Bad News. These congregations will probably not reach very far beyond their comfort zone and will most likely be populated with people like them. Wise pastors will look for ways to confess the Bad News without starting a war. But this move cannot be omitted. If we think bad news never had a place among the worshiping people of God, we need to think again.

Read the lament psalms. Try Pss. 77, 88, and 137. These are raw expressions of the Bad News. Some of them recite the world's speeches. When's the last time you read those psalms in church? These psalms were acts of worship.

Some "praise and worship" congregations habitually

refuse to engage the Bad News. If I have any critique for the praise and worship movement, it is the avoidance of the Bad News. When all our songs are up and happy, the down and sad among us have no place to express how their lives are really going. People who've had a hard week stay home because they can't stand to be among all those happy people. The crowd of apparently successful Christians intimidates people who've failed. People with doubts are permitted no place to ask the same questions asked by Job, Peter, Mary, Thomas, and Jesus. In the Bad News, we can question God as Job did. We can deal with our denials of Jesus as Peter did. We can say with Mary, "How can this be?" (Luke 1:34). We can doubt right alongside Thomas. And we can cry out with Jesus, "My God, my God, why have you forsaken me?" (Matt. 27:46). We do not chase the Bad News away by not mentioning it in our worship gatherings. We merely drive it underground to fester in the soul. When we name the Bad News in the presence of God, we open ourselves to help.

The Bad News can take 5 to 10 minutes or longer if it bleeds into the opening of the sermon. You are looking for a congregational nod of recognition. This happens when the people collectively say, "This is true. Life in the world really is like that. And we wish it could be different." A congregation located (Entrance) in the presence of God and honest about the Bad News is now in a good place to hear the gospel (Good News).

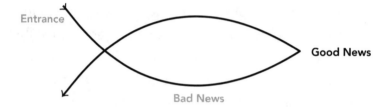

Entrance

Good News

Bad News

ACT III
The Good News

Here's where we shine! We love to declare good news:

"We're engaged!"

"Guess what! You're going to be a grandfather!"

"The tumor is benign."

"You have the job."

"We don't have to move."

"Yes, I'd love to go out on a date with you!"

Good news. We long to hear it. If it is credible, it changes us.

The Bible is full of good news:

"I have heard your cry" (see Exod. 3:7).

"Let my people go" (Exod. 5:1).

"You meant it for harm, but God meant it for good" (see Gen. 50:20).

"Forgive them" (Luke 23:34).

"The father ran to meet him" (see Luke 15:20).

"Behold, I am coming soon" (see Rev. 22:20).

Every one of these statements has a story. Every announcement of good news is made in the context of bad news. Can you imagine declaring to a lunch group, "I've got good news. It's benign." They would assume you were tested for cancer, or that someone close to you had received a report. Without a context of threatened disease, this good news makes no sense at all. This is why the Bad News of worship is so critical to the announcement of Good News. The Bad News, Act II, allows the Good News, Act III, to become the climax of the worship drama, the turning point from bad to good.

For most congregations, the reading of Scripture and the sermon constitute the Good News. But the acts of worship do not always end and begin cleanly with service components. Sometimes the Bad News bridges from a speech about greed to a story of a man who built bigger and bigger barns or a tax collector who ripped people off. But halfway through these texts, the turn toward the Good News was made. Sometimes the opening five minutes of a sermon is all bad news. The preacher is analyzing sin, and the people are agreeing. The Good News has not arrived yet, but it's on its way.

The Good News must come. Prophets eventually got to the good news. Jesus went from bad-news town to bad-news town preaching the gospel, which means the Good News. Paul went into the Gentile world (a bad-news setting) preaching the good news of Jesus. A service in which the Bad News dominates, or in which the Good News never makes an appearance, is not a Christian service. Preaching is the declaration of the Good News incarnated in Jesus, the One sent from God into a world that didn't know God.

Our worship is centered on God and informed by Scripture. The Entrance, Bad News, and Good News all sit down in front of the text of the day and ask key questions of it. The Entrance asks, "What is God like in this text? What is being revealed here about God?" The Bad News asks, "How are humans in trouble? What has gone wrong here?" The Good News asks, "What hope or help is being offered here? What gift is God giving? What is God up to?" The answers to these questions begin to guide our choices in constructing a worship experience for people.

As I was writing this chapter, I came to this point and wrote, "Gone are the days when people will show up to be harassed, harangued, and hamstrung by angry preachers wearing toe-stomping holy boots." But I crossed it out. I don't think those days are over. One of the characteristics of religious fundamentalism is an incessant focus on the Bad News. People flock to sanctuaries to hear scathing condemnations of homosexuals and liberal politicians. They feed on anger against enemies—real and imagined. The service does not succeed, in their minds, unless the attack has been severe and thorough.

My fear is that these gatherings, repeated week after

week, harden us in an anger that is deep, a lifestyle that is escapist, and a gospel that is mostly bad news. People who define good worship as "stomping on toes until it hurts" need to take a fresh look at the ministry of Jesus. The only toes He consistently stepped on were those sandaled in religion.

I am not saying we should not name sin as sin or avoid practicing the prophetic art of challenging the world's ways. This is exactly what is done in the Bad News act of worship. I am calling for that radical transition somewhere around sermon time that smiles ear to ear and asks, "Would you like to hear God's good news for people like us in a world like this?" I am convinced that people will attend churches that are honest about the Bad News and excited about the Good News.

We would tire of a medical doctor who went on and on about the nature of our disease but never got to the cure. We would run out of patience with the auto mechanic who jabbered (at $35 per hour) about the problem with our carburetor but never talked about repair. We grow numb under preaching that drones on and on about sin in a dark world but never gets to transforming grace.

Preaching the Good News is vision casting. It is the God-called, God-inspired art of offering people a preferred picture of the future. We learn this from the prophets. They stood with one foot firmly planted in the mess of their day and the other in the tomorrow that God alone could create. They were vision casters. They offered a hopeful future to people mired in sin. They envisioned people healed, restored, forgiven, and cleansed.

Most of the stories of Scripture are cast in a bad-news/good-news tension:

Bad News	Good News
We were slaves in Egypt (see Deut. 6:21).	God says, "Let my people go" (Exod. 5:1).
We are thirsty.	"I am the water of life" (see John 4).
The prodigal left home.	The father ran out to meet him (see Luke 15).
"I was blind."	"Now I see" (John 9:25).
She had bled for 12 years.	When she touched Jesus' garment, she was healed (see Matt. 9:20-22).
Once we were not a people.	Now we are the people of God (see 1 Pet. 2:10).

Like a seesaw, these stories are carefully balanced with Bad News and Good News. Give them each their due. Tell the whole story. And spend plenty of time on the Good News.

Timing the Acts of Worship

How much weight do you give to each of these acts? In a one-hour worship gathering, how long should each take?

As mentioned earlier, the Entrance can take 5 to 10

minutes. The process of locating people in the presence of God should be long enough to celebrate the kind of God being revealed in the text of the morning. It should contain a heavy dose of the welcoming hospitality of God. People should have no doubt where they are.

The Bad News, as we've also observed, can take 5 to 10 minutes or longer if it bleeds into the opening of the sermon. Get to the point. Look for the congregation's acknowledgment that you have been truthful about the sinful condition of the world. Be honest.

The Good News should begin within 20 to 25 minutes into the service and should take 20 to 30 minutes. In most services, the sermon is the bulk of the service. And sadly, it is often disconnected from anything else that happens. By placing the sermon somewhere in the range of 20 minutes after the beginning of the service to 15 minutes till its end, there is plenty of time for the last two acts of worship—the Response of the People and the Blessing.

A service that has the preacher roaring to a screeching sermonic halt at the end of the hour often cheats a congregation out of an appropriate response. This is best remedied by planning the first 20 minutes of the service rather than rushing the last few minutes.

Let's summarize. You've come into the presence of God in the Entrance that locates you. You've nodded in recognition that the news from our world is bad. You've heard what God, in Christ, has done to offer us freedom

and hope. What next? You are ready to respond to the
Good News.

ACT IV
The Response of the People

The doctor tells you the bad news. She explains the medical procedures for your illness. Now it's your turn. The responsibility is placed in your lap. Do you wish to be healed?

Likewise, the mechanic lays out the problem, suggests the repair, and estimates the cost. Now it's your turn. Yes or no? Fix it or drive an at-risk automobile?

The worship plot brings us to the place of response. This is not a response that we initiate, but one we are made capable of by the activity of God. In recognizing where we are (Entrance), what is wrong (Bad News), and where hope lies (Good News), we have been opened by God to God for grace. Now we are ready for Act IV of our drama, the falling action. In a play this is where the main character's response to a positive climax should draw the story to a pleasing outcome. In worship, our response to the Good News should do the same.

I am deeply indebted to Willow Creek Church and Bill Hybels, its founding pastor. From these good people, I learned how to sharpen the bad-news/good-news acts in a service. I learned relevancy, honesty, and how to see the world through lost eyes. However, the one issue I have with their work is the label *seeker-sensitive.* The primary seeker is God. We do not open our hearts to God on our own. God opens us. God seeks us. God loves us. He is the active seeker in a service. In designing worship, we plot a way to accompany God in search of lost and broken people. Rather than viewing humans as seeking after God, we view God as seeking humans. Unless this distinction is made, a service can be designed to manipulate human response. (I want to be very clear in saying that worship leaders at Willow Creek are not manipulative. The passion of God for lost people drives their choices. I only express my opinion that the *seeker-sensitive* label is more descriptive of God than people.)

This fourth act of the worship plot, the Response of the People, finds its cue in Scripture. In the same way we asked questions of the text to determine the first three acts, we do the same here. We ask, "What human response is implied or desired in this text? What should people do in light of this good news?" The answer to these questions will suggest ways a congregation might respond. This is not to limit the response in any way but to clear the way for people to respond verbally and bodily to God's gracious offer. The responses are many and varied:

- Repent of sin.
- Be baptized.
- Be anointed for healing.
- Sing our commitment.
- Volunteer for service.
- Give money.
- Kneel in submission to God.
- Write a note of encouragement.
- Pray for sanctification.
- Dedicate an infant.
- Listen for God's voice of discernment regarding an issue.
- Affirm another believer in a time of grieving.
- Receive the Lord's Supper.
- Ask forgiveness of a spouse.
- Break bread.
- Wash feet.
- Pray for the sick.
- Make a decision and note it on a card.
- Give a public testimony.

These are some of the ways we respond to the gospel. Rather than exiting the service at the end of a sermon, we move in obedience together. We model response. We are not people who listen to the Word and go away unchanged.

James calls us to response:

Be doers of the word, and not merely hearers who

deceive themselves. For if any are hearers of the word and not doers, they are like those who look at themselves in a mirror; for they look at themselves and, on going away, immediately forget what they were like. But those who look into the perfect law, the law of liberty, and persevere, being not hearers who forget but doers who act—they will be blessed in their doing *(James 1:22-25)*.

Obedient response is the only appropriate response to the gospel.

As we hear the Bad News and the Good News, something is happening. We are either being hardened or being opened. The Word of God causes effect. Some are blinded, made deaf, and hardened in their hearts. Others are being saved. The Word of God does not allow us to remain neutral.

Indeed, the word of God is living and active, sharper than any two-edged sword, piercing until it divides soul from spirit, joints from marrow; it is able to judge the thoughts and intentions of the heart. And before him no creature is hidden, but all are naked and laid bare to the eyes of the one to whom we must render an account *(Heb. 4:12-13)*.

In the same chapter, the writer urges the people, "Today, if you hear his voice, do not harden your hearts" (v. 7).

A human response will occur when the Word is preached. We do not need to manipulate that response.

Contrived human response is a lack of confidence in the power of the Spirit. The cutting edge of the Good News moves people off dead center. In one direction the heart grows colder and harder. In the other, we are opened to experience the grace of God in some measure.

A strong belief in prevenient grace leads us to recognize the activity of God in pre-Christians. Those who have not experienced conversion can experience the grace of God leading them toward spiritual life. In our services, we often ask people who have not become Christians to pray this prayer: "God, I am willing to be made aware of Your love for me. Open my eyes to see You at work in my life. Take away the blinders that have kept me in spiritual darkness. As yet, I do not believe, but I am willing to be opened to the possibility." This prayer offers nonbelievers an opportunity to respond to the gospel in a way that moves them toward openness.

Everyone should have an opportunity to respond. If, Sunday after Sunday, the only public response offered is the invitation to come forward to pray, we excuse most of the congregation. We train 90 percent or more of the church that no response is needed.

One Sunday, our congregation was working on the issue of reconciliation with family members. The Entrance focused on the God of reconciliation. The Bad News reminded us that the people closest to us often inflict life's deepest wounds. The Good News rose out of the story of

Joseph, despised and sold into slavery by his brothers. The sermon title was "Outliving What Your Family Did to You." In a powerful scene of love and reconciliation, Joseph reveals himself to his brothers and testifies to God's grace in his life. When we came to the Response of the People, it would have been easy to close the service with the suggestion that we all go make peace with those who had hurt us. We took it a step deeper. We provided paper and pens and asked people to spend time writing a letter of reconciliation on the spot. For 10 minutes all you could hear was the sound of ballpoint pen on hymnal-backed paper. Tears flowed as many wrote letters to those in their family who had wounded them. They wrote to the music of the gentle prayer, "Lord, make me an instrument of Thy peace." Then we sang the Lord's Prayer, "Forgive us our debts, as we forgive our debtors" (Matt. 6:9-13, KJV).

When people hear the gospel and respond immediately, the word takes root. Obedience becomes natural. When they hear it and walk away having done nothing, the chance for transformation is diminished.

"Listen! A sower went out to sow. And as he sowed, some seed fell on the path, and the birds came and ate it up. Other seed fell on rocky ground, where it did not have much soil, and it sprang up quickly, since it had no depth of soil. And when the sun rose, it was scorched; and since it had no root, it withered away. Other seed fell among thorns, and the thorns grew up and choked it, and it yielded no grain. Other seed fell into good soil and brought forth grain, growing up and increasing and yielding thirty and sixty and a hundredfold." And he said, "Let anyone with ears to hear listen!" When he was alone, those who were around him along with the twelve asked him about the parables. And he said to them, "To you has been given the secret of the kingdom of God, but for those outside, everything comes in parables; in order that 'they may indeed look, but not perceive, and may indeed listen, but not understand; so that they may not turn again and be forgiven.'" And he said to them, "Do you not understand this parable? . . . The sower sows the word. These are the ones on the path where the word is sown: when they hear, Satan immediately comes and takes away the word that is sown in them. And these are the ones sown on rocky ground: when they hear the word, they immediately receive it with joy. But they have no root, and endure only for a while; then, when trouble or persecution arises on account of the word, immediately they fall away. And others are those sown among the thorns: these are the ones who hear the world, but the cares of the world, and the lure of wealth, and the desire for other things come in and choke the word, and it yields nothing. And these are the ones sown on the good soil: they hear the word and accept it and bear fruit, thirty and sixty and a hundredfold" *(Mark 4:3-20)*.

The fruit of the word is wrapped up in the God-enabled response of the people.

When Jesus walked into bad-news settings to deliver good news, He called for a response:

- "Follow me" (Matt. 4:19).
- "Come down. I'm going to eat with you" (see Luke 19:5).
- "Sell your possessions" (Matt. 19:21).
- "Forgive your brother from the heart" (Matt. 18:35, NIV).
- "Go, and sin no more" (John 8:11, KJV).
- "Repent and believe. The promise is for you" (see Acts 2:38-39).
- "Be baptized" (Acts 2:38).
- "Eat the bread. Drink the cup. Remember me" (see 1 Cor. 11).
- "Go. Make disciples" (see Matt. 28:19).

The Good News calls for a response. This response needs to be as sensual as possible. The more we taste, touch, see, feel, and hear, the more engaged we are in responding. Our bodies are capable of such a response. We can love God with heart, soul, mind, and strength. We have much to learn from other traditions. The sacramental churches can teach us to use bread, water, grape juice, oil, candles, incense, and rose petals. The Pentecostal traditions can teach us to use our hands, feet, and hips. The Quakers can teach us to get quiet and listen. The gospel calls for the most embodied response we are capable of. And the response fits the Good News.

I grew up in southern camp meetings. The old Sartinsville Camp Meeting in Mississippi is a place of reverence in my memory. I think we were closer to this idea of human response then than we are now. The sermon occupied the middle part of the service. Following the sermon came a long altar invitation. The invitation was offered to the lost, to those seeking sanctification, to the sick, to the discouraged. Several different needs were addressed. Oil came out and people were anointed. Testimonies were shared, and people clapped for the joy of victory. Thanksgiving was expressed for an answer to a long-term prayer. Love offerings were taken, and people broke out in spontaneous choruses of praise. The Response of the People often lasted for 30 to 60 minutes. While there is a lot about camp meeting days I do not wish to recover, the Response of the People is one thing I'd love to bring back.

In a one-hour service, it is possible to plan for time to respond. If the sermon concludes no later than 15 minutes till the hour, there is time for prayer, offering, singing, and other responses. Congregational singing does not all need to be in the Entrance. Some songs are more meaningful as a Response of the People. About 15 to 20 minutes of response makes the event participatory. This worship move rescues us from the tendency to entertain spectators. It asks something from those who come. It is liturgical, which means "the work of the people."

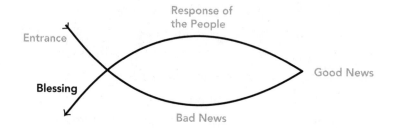

ACT V
The Blessing

"You wanna know why I come to church?" she asked me.

"Sure," I replied.

"I come for the blessing. When you raise your hands at the end of the service and say those good words, well . . . it's the only time something like that happens to me during the week. Everywhere else I get dumped on. When you bless us, I feel like I can live another week."

I'll never forget that conversation. The young woman was right. Blessing is what I call it—the benediction, good words. And it doesn't take long. Maybe two minutes max. But it is important. Like the conclusion or denouement in a play where the main character ends up in better circumstances than at the start, so it is with the Blessing and us. We hear we are better off in light of the Good News and our positive response to God's grace. We are sent out into the world under the blessing of God. We depart to serve under His smile and favor, invigorated by His Spirit. We are going out where Jesus goes, as children of the Father. The Trinity is at work in us.

Most of the New Testament letters end with a blessing. Hebrews concludes by saying,

> Now may the God of peace, who brought back from the dead our Lord Jesus, the great shepherd of the sheep, by the blood of the eternal covenant, make you complete in everything good so that you may do his will, working among us that which is pleasing in his sight, through Jesus Christ, to whom be the glory forever and ever. Amen *(13:20-22)*.

Philippians ends,

> The grace of the Lord Jesus Christ be with your spirit *(4:23)*.

Paul's second letter to Corinth concludes with,

> The grace of the Lord Jesus Christ, the love of God, and the communion of the Holy Spirit be with all of you *(13:13)*.

Other commonly used scriptural blessings are printed in hymnals. Some can be sung to or by the people: "The Lord Bless You and Keep You," "Sent Forth by God's Blessing," "Forth in the Peace of Christ We Go," "God Be with You."

The scripture text for the day may contain a blessing waiting to be discovered. In the service on reconciling with a family member who has wronged you, we allowed people to write letters of reconciling peace. The benediction for the morning was, "May the Spirit of God accompany your words of peace to the heart of one estranged. May the presence of Jesus come alongside during its reading. And may the Father make of us brothers and sisters, members of one family. Go in peace."

The Blessing is empowering. It reminds people that God is at work in their response and will be at work in their world. It gives boldness to beaten-down people. It whispers gracious words to those who hear grumbling all week long. It invades damaged esteem with the Creator's value. It counters the curses of the world.

In Scripture, a blessing is words with the power to do good. A curse is words with the power to harm. The world curses us. The world speaks to us in ways that steal, kill, and destroy. The world's words manipulate us for selfish gain. God's words of blessing counter the curse.

It may seem a small thing to do, but God moves in a blessing upon His people.

May the God who gathers us for worship grant those of us who are worship leaders grace to lead His people into their story.

SAMPLES AND MORE

A.
Sample Series

The people from Missouri are known to say, "Show me." In this section, I want to walk you through a three-week series we did at College Church of the Nazarene in Bourbonnais, Illinois. The first Sunday is fully developed —drama, sermon, and script. The second week is an abbreviated worship plot. The third week is a picture of a working worship plot 8 weeks prior to the service. The theme of the series is "Holy Habits Rarely Seen." The texts are drawn from the Gospel of Luke. We looked at the kinds of things Jesus did that are rarely done by His people today. These include eating with unlikely strangers, exorcism, and praying properly.

These themes were developed in August. Musicians and dramatists had 10 weeks to work on the plot line of the service. Linda Stone, a volunteer in our drama ministry, wrote most of the dramas. Some of the humor in the dramas is local. When we use a published drama, we try to rescript it with a local flair. One of the weaknesses of prepackaged services and sermons is the absence of context. We have learned not to import drama or sermons from other sources without running it through our local context grid. This unmasks my bias against sermons that are bought, borrowed, or begged from other sources. Sterile outlines in a magazine begin in another world, not the world of the worshiping congregation at hand. Home-cooked sermons lend themselves to home-cooked services, which fit the ethos and appetite of the home crowd.

WEEK ONE

Holy Habits Rarely Seen:
Eating with Unlikely People

Entrance

As you come into the sanctuary, you hear someone playing a saxophone, accompanied by the band. It's a Dixieland rendition of "When the Saints Go Marching In." You find yourself in a toe-tapping mood. Someone steps to center stage and says,

Good morning. What a great thought . . . to be included in the crowd that goes marching into heaven. I want to be in that number when the saints go marching in. They are headed to a banquet. And when it comes to mealtime, no one wants to be left out. It's our hope that our visitors don't feel left out this morning. You'll find a visitor's card in the pew rack in front of you. If you'd like more information about the life and ministries of College Church, fill that out and drop it in the offering plate when it passes. We don't expect that you came prepared to participate in the offering, so feel free to take a pass. Just drop the card in the plate. We promise not to put you on an eternal mailing list. We only want to deliver a packet of information designed to introduce you to us. We are learning to be hospitable and inclusive. God is our Teacher. He loves everybody. We're glad you're here.

The music team is already in place. Our music leader invites people to stand and sing. We sing about the love of God for all His creatures. In our contemporary service we sing "His Love Reaches," "It's the Sweet, Sweet, Sweet Presence of Jesus," and "Think About His Love." In a more traditional service we sing "The Love of God," "Such Love," and "Think About His Love." The songs focus us on the inclusive heart of God. A prayer is offered, thanking God for grace extended to people like us. Before people are seated, they greet those around them.

Bad News

As people are greeting each other, the platform is set for the drama. The setting is two lunch tables on opposite sides of the platform. At one table, three people wrestle with life issues. They have no faith or understanding of God's grace toward them. Oblivious to this conversation, three believers at the other table talk about life issues from the perspective of their faith. The conversation and spotlight shift from one table to the other sequentially. You find yourself wishing that these people could eat together. The drama ends with each group meeting at the trash can in the center. You realize that these people work together every day and eat in the same lunchroom. But they never mix company over a meal.

Table for Six
by
Linda Stone

Scene

Two tables with three people at each. They're eating lunch. Some of them brown-bagged. The Christians sit at one table, the non-Christians at the other. (I tried to give them fairly genderless names to make casting a little easier, but some lines might have to be changed.)

Table 1—Christians	Table 2—Non-Christians
CHRIS	PHIL/PHYLLIS
ROBIN	SAM/SAMANTHA
DANA	GENE/JEAN

(Lights up on Table 1)

CHRIS *(sighs):* Another Monday. *(Starts opening Tupperware)*

ROBIN: It sure is. You brought lunch? You're ambitious. What is it?

CHRIS: Leftover Sunday pot roast, of course. And it's not ambition; it's end-of-the-month poverty.

DANA: Wow, you guys still have pot roast on Sundays?

CHRIS: Just like mom used to make.

ROBIN: Dinner at your house next week! We had peanut butter and jelly.

CHRIS: On a Sunday?

ROBIN: Yeah. By the time we got home from church, that's all I had time for. We had promised my mother-in-law we'd bring the kids over to rake leaves in the afternoon.

DANA: How's she doing?

ROBIN: Better. She has a lot of friends from church who are keeping her busy. I know she still misses my father-in-law like crazy, but at least she's not home alone too much.

DANA: They say that it's the weeks and months after the funeral, when life gets quiet again, that are the hardest.

ROBIN: She and my father-in-law were on a lot of peoples' prayer lists in the months before he died, and those people are still there for her.

CHRIS: I don't know how people do it, without the grace of God and the support of Christian friends. Some people face death without a clue that God even exists. I don't know how they make it.

DANA *(shaking head):* I don't either.

(Lights out on Table 1, up on Table 2)

PHIL: So, how was everybody's weekend?

GENE: Too short, as usual.

SAM: Mine was too long.

PHIL: I didn't know that was possible.

SAM: It is if you're at a funeral.

PHIL: Oh, I'm sorry. Who was it?

SAM: My wife's cousin. She died in an accident. The whole family is pretty torn up.

GENE: Did you spend the whole weekend with them?

SAM: Pretty much; had some out-of-town relatives staying with us. We had to split them up—you know, somebody's not speaking to somebody else; this one hurt that one's feelings 10 years ago. As if the reason we were all there wasn't bad enough. *(Pauses)* What I wouldn't give to have seen a friendly face around there.

PHIL: How old was the cousin?

SAM: She was 35.

GENE: Man. Really makes you think.

SAM: Yep. Sure does. My wife is taking it pretty bad. She and her cousin were pretty close—like sisters. And I don't know how to help her. She's been really quiet—too quiet. When she does talk to me, she has all these questions about life . . . I mean, what am I supposed to say? I sure don't have the answers. *(Shakes his head)* Thirty-five!

PHIL: Thirty-five. I guess you never know, huh?

SAM *(slowly, thoughtfully):* Nope . . . you never do.

(Lights out on Table 2, up on Table 1)

ROBIN: Well, I didn't know Monday lunch was going to turn out to be testimony time, but I have to tell you guys something. I found out Saturday that my sister and her husband are getting back together.

DANA: Really? I never thought that would happen!

CHRIS: Why? What's the story on your sister?

ROBIN: She and her husband have been separated for over a year. Very bitter divorce in the works—the only thing holding it up was the question of custody—neither of them wanted to hurt the kids.

CHRIS: And now they're getting back together?

ROBIN: Yes. They started going to counseling to work on helping the kids deal with the divorce and ended up deciding maybe it wasn't over after all.

DANA: Wow. God really does answer prayer. You were praying for them long before they split up—I think you knew they were in trouble before they did.

Robin: It's nothing short of a miracle. And they'd be the first ones to admit it was God at work in their lives. This was not something they figured out how to fix on their own.

Dana (to Chris): She's not kidding. You should have seen these two. Once they had a shouting match in front of Robin's house.

(Lights out on Table 1, up on Table 2)

Gene: So then my wife tells him she can go out. After I just told him he was grounded. She thinks I'm too hard on him; I think she's too soft. I'm telling you, this kid is pushing us apart!

Phil: And he's probably making the most of it. They're experts at that age. Divide and conquer.

Gene: Tell me about it. I don't think we'll ever even argue once that kid is out of the house. If we make it that long.

Sam: Hang in there. About the time they turn human again, they leave.

Phil: Tell that to my 25-year-old daughter.

Gene: Aw, I don't even want to hear that.

Phil: It's not so bad. With her around, my wife has someone to shop with. I haven't had to go to the mall in years.

GENE: I get so desperate for peace and quiet, I'd even be willing to go to the mall with my wife. But I don't think she'd want me to. Sometimes I'm afraid we don't have anything in common anymore. Or won't once the kids are gone.

SAM: Is it really that bad?

GENE: Well . . . remember a few weeks ago when she went to Michigan for the weekend? The weekend stretched into two weeks and I, uh . . . I wasn't sure she was coming home. And she wasn't sure either.

PHIL: But she did come back.

GENE: Yeah, she's there, but . . . *(Looks like he wants to say more, but just shakes his head)*

SAM: Maybe you two should talk to somebody.

GENE *(reluctant):* I don't know, maybe . . . I wouldn't know where to start. I mean, who wants to listen to someone else's marriage problems?

(Lights out on Table 2, up on Table 1)

CHRIS: There have been a lot of times when I didn't know how we'd get through something, but God really does give you the grace when you need it, and not ahead of time.

DANA: True. Sometimes I wish . . . *(hesitates)*

ROBIN: What? Go ahead. . . .

DANA: Well, I don't want to sound like I know it all, but sometimes I wish there was a way for me to share what I've learned. I'd really like to help people going through hard times.

CHRIS: I'm sure they'd let you take a Sunday School class or even some kind of support group.

ROBIN: But see, there you'd be, still in the church. Sometimes I feel like our lives revolve so much around church activities that I don't even know anybody who's not a Christian.

DANA: I know what you mean. All our friends are there; it seems like we spend every weekend there, the kids are involved . . .

(Lights go up on both tables; DANA and GENE speak simultaneously)

GENE and DANA: I just wish I knew who to talk to about it.

(Everybody starts looking at their watches; somebody says it's one o'clock and they'd better get back to work. All six rise and start putting their trash in the same trash can, nodding hello to each other, etc., and we realize [hopefully] that they all work at the same place and are together every day.)

(Lights out)

Good News: The Sermon

The preacher walks onto the platform and stands between the two lunch tables and begins the sermon:

Of all the places habits can be observed, the dinner table may be the best. Eating reveals our habits:

- Where we sit.
- Saying grace.
- "Pass the salt, please."
- Using the correct fork.
- Smacking the lips.
- Interrupting.
- Lecturing.
- Placing your napkin in your lap.

Eating reveals habits.

In Luke's Gospel, Jesus comes strolling into a world made new by His presence. He sees things differently and behaves differently. His habits shatter the prevailing culture. He practices habits rarely seen. And of all the possible places to introduce new habits, Jesus chooses the table.

Julia Child wouldn't have done what He did. Gloria Vanderbilt wouldn't have done what He did. The truth is, we are very hesitant to do what He did.

What did He do? Well, to understand that, I'll need to tell you a little about meals and tables in Luke's day. There were four rules.

1. Meals were the way you managed the bound-

aries of your life. On normal days, your family gathered at your table. On special occasions you might extend the boundary to include others. Through meal invitations, you declared who belonged and who didn't. Rule No. 1 sounds familiar.

2. Where you sat at a meal ranked you socially. As a guest at a meal, the closer you sat to the host, the higher your status. The further you sat from the host, the lower your status. You could tell the pecking order of the community by observing the seating pattern. Rule No. 2 isn't so strange to us either. I remember hearing one of our daughters arranging the seating for her birthday party. Best friends near. Barely invited friends, down at the other end of the table. And who among us doesn't try to arrive early at open seating banquets? We don't want to get stuck eating with "certain" people all evening.

3. Meals were to be reciprocated. If you invite me, I am obligated to return the favor. It isn't a courtesy; it's a must. So this means I am going to be very careful about accepting an invitation from you because, after all, do I really want to reciprocate?

4. You only invited people who could affirm or improve your social standing. Your A-list included people who were higher than you in social standing. It took courage to invite them because they might refuse your invitation due to the obligation to invite

you back. Your B-list included people who were on your level. This was a safe invite. Your C-list was comprised of people you wouldn't think of inviting. They would drag you down.

It would be easy to throw rocks at these rules, but this is just how it was. People were picky about table guests. People preferred the better seats. People excused themselves from invitations that obligated them. People thought of each other in pecking-order fashion.

Into that world, Jesus comes teaching:

> On one occasion when Jesus was going to the house of a leader of the Pharisees to eat a meal on the sabbath, they were watching him closely. Just then, in front of him, there was a man who had dropsy. And Jesus asked the lawyers and Pharisees, "Is it lawful to cure people on the sabbath, or not?" But they were silent. So Jesus took him and healed him, and sent him away. Then he said to them, "If one of you has a child or an ox that has fallen into a well, will you not immediately pull it out on a sabbath day?" And they could not reply to this *(Luke 14:1-6)*.

Apparently Jesus had taught in the synagogue on the Sabbath. He was a visitor en route to Jerusalem. The leading Pharisee thought Him worth the risk of a dinner invitation. But being the new guy, the Phar-

isees were watching Him closely. On the way to dinner, Jesus came face-to-face with a bloated man. His
body was retaining too much fluid. The curse of
dropsy is an insatiable craving for water coupled with
the inability to void the water. This guy is killing himself with fluid, and his body is screaming for more.
He craves the very thing he already has too much of.
Jesus asks permission to heal him. The dinner party is
dumbfounded. Not a word of reply. Jesus healed him
and sent him home, explaining that they would have
done the same for a cow or a kid. Again, no reply. But
I'm guessing they were thinking bad things about
their dinner guest.

When he noticed how the guests chose the
places of honor, he told them a parable. "When
you are invited by someone to a wedding banquet, do not sit down at the place of honor, in
case someone more distinguished than you has
been invited by your host; and the host who invited both of you may come and say to you, 'Give
this person your place,' and then in disgrace you
would start to take the lowest place. But when
you are invited, go and sit down at the lowest
place, so that when your host comes, he may say
to you, 'Friend, move up higher'; then you will be
honored in the presence of all who sit at the table
with you. For all who exalt themselves will be

humbled, and those who humble themselves will be exalted" *(vv. 7-11)*.

They had been watching Jesus to see what He would do. Now Jesus watches them scramble for the best seats in the house. They probably remind Jesus of the bloated man—an insatiable thirst for what they already had plenty of. They were bloated with status and didn't know how to void it from themselves. Their bodies screamed for more. They wanted the seat of honor worse than the sick man wanted a drink. Jesus, being an equal-opportunity healer, offered a cure. Take the worst seat in the house. Instead of testing the pecking order, take the risk of humility. Accept your status as a gift from the host. Hope that the host will "call you up."

All through Luke's Gospel, God does this—calls people up, from low to high, from down to up, from last to first. Jesus is suggesting a new dining habit. Rather than vie for status, receive it as the free gift of God.

If you are thinking about saying "Amen" right here, think twice. Are we really ready to embrace this habit? We compete with each other for place:

- Not everyone stands on the medal podium at the Olympics.
- Only one person will be elected president.
- Not everyone gets promoted.

- There are bell curves.
- GPAs separate us.
- At graduation there are three kinds of laudes.
- In tournaments, you hope for first, second, or third places.
- Miss America is chosen from 50, then 10, then 5—and nobody remembers the runner-up.
- We have income brackets and social standings.

You don't get far in this world by willingly taking last place. The Chicago Cubs have tried this for years, and no one ever invites them to the World Series. They don't get called up.

What Jesus is suggesting is social suicide. He is out of step with the way our culture operates. His table habit would make everyone in his or her right mind think He had lost His.

But then, could this really cure dropsy? Could it cure the thirst for status that bloats us? Could we survive by receiving honor as a gift rather than wrenching it from each other? It's worth a thought.

As our text continues, you'll see that Jesus is an equal-opportunity offender. Having addressed the guests about their game of "power musical chairs," He now turns to talk to the host about the guest list.

He said also to the one who had invited him, "When you give a luncheon or dinner, do not invite your friends or your brothers or your relatives or rich neighbors, in case they may invite you in return, and you would be repaid. But when you give a banquet, invite the poor, the crippled, the lame, and the blind. And you will be blessed, because they cannot repay you, for you will be repaid at the resurrection of the righteous" *(vv. 12-14)*.

Have you ever had the audacity to tell your host that he invited the wrong people to dinner? Jesus suggests to the host that he scrap his A-list and his B-list and go straight to his Z-list. The Z-list doesn't even exist in the host's imagination. The poor, crippled, lame, and blind aren't on anyone's list. They can't add to your status. They cost you points. They can't pay you back. Inviting them would be pure mercy.

You may be thinking about saying "Amen" right here, but think twice. Our world doesn't work this way:

- Financial planners don't work a crowd of bums.
- College professors don't have coffee with high school dropouts.
- Coaches don't frequent hospitals looking for recruits.
- Graduating college students don't list jobless people as references.
- Pastors don't inquire about an opening at a small church full of needy people.
- Doctors don't open a practice in the blighted area of town.

We connect with the people who can help us. We rarely lower the boundaries of our life to people who have absolutely nothing to contribute to who we are. This habit would go unrewarded everywhere in the world—with the exception of the resurrection of the righteous.

Apparently, one of the dinner guests wants to change the drift of the conversation. Jesus' talk about a resurrection of the righteous reminds him of a saying:

> One of the dinner guests, on hearing this, said to him, "Blessed is anyone who will eat bread in the kingdom of God!" Then Jesus said to him, "Someone gave a great dinner and invited many. At the time for the dinner he sent his slave to say to those who had been invited, 'Come; for everything is ready now.' But they all alike began to make excuses. The first said to him, 'I have bought a piece of land, and I must go out and see it; please accept my regrets.' Another said, 'I have bought five yoke of oxen, and I am going to try them out; please accept my regrets.' Another said, 'I have just been married, and therefore I cannot come.' So the slave returned and reported this to his master. Then the owner of the house became angry and said to his slave, 'Go out at once into the streets and lanes of the town and bring in the poor, the crippled, the blind, and the lame.' And

the slave said, 'Sir, what you ordered has been done, and there is still room.' Then the master said to the slave, 'Go out into the roads and lanes, and compel people to come in, so that my house may be filled. For I tell you, none of those who were invited will taste my dinner'" *(vv. 15-24)*.

The unthinkable has happened. An important man has sent out invitations for a great dinner, and all the guests are excusing themselves. This is a social disaster. With each RSVP, his status stock is plummeting. The invitees are wrenching from the host his standing in the community. It is social assassination. What is the host to do?

Maybe he tries out Jesus' new dinner habit. Invite the Z-list—the poor, the crippled, the lame, the blind. But you'll have to bring them. They won't come on their own. You'll have to convince them they're invited. They won't believe their ears. They'll think it's a cruel joke and they're being set up for a shaming. You'll have to compel them, because they know they can't reciprocate your invitation. What's that? There's still room at the table?

Response of the People

(The pastor walks to the Communion table, beautifully decorated with bread, grapes, and chalice.)

And this brings us to this Communion table. How

did you *(looking inquisitively at the gathered congregation)* get on the invitation list? I know you. You are not righteous enough to merit an invitation. You can't improve God's social standing. People like you will cost God points if word gets out that you were on the list. And there are no seats around this table. How will we know who is important here? And how will we reciprocate God for this invitation? Can we produce a meal that equals this one? I see Z-list people sitting here this morning. Some of you are probably shocked to discover your name on the list. It comes as a surprise to you that this is no cruel joke. God really does mean to include you in His banquet. It is His intent that you be in that number when the saints go marching in.

Too good to be true? Yes.

Any requirements? Yes. There are two meal rules:

1. You must come hungry, open to receive life as the free gift of God. This is not something you earned.

2. You must be breathing.

Let's bow to say grace.

"Gracious God, these are Your gifts to Your people. The body and blood of Your Son, Jesus, is our life. We come to this table having examined ourselves in the light of Your grace. We are needy. We are hungry. We are open for the forgiveness, healing, and cleansing that comes from fellowship with You at this table. Bless this food to the nourishment of our body and soul. Amen."

As a worshiper, you are invited to stand and come forward to a central table at the front. You are with other believers gathered around three sides of the table as you take the bread and cup. You eat and drink, looking into the faces of fellow worshipers. This takes 10 to 15 minutes for everyone to come to the table and eat. During this time, you are singing "Make Us One, Lord," "The Servant Song," "Give Thanks," "You Are My All in All," "Let Us Break Bread Together."

Blessing

How do we reciprocate such a gift? By going from this table to live in the grace and acceptance of God. By eating with the unlikely people of our world. By extending our table boundaries to include anyone God directs us to. By remembering how it feels to be included in the kingdom of grace.

The Lord bless you and keep you. The Lord be with you at each meal and open your eyes to His presence. The Lord make holy the tables throughout this city in the week to come. Amen.

WEEK TWO
Holy Habits Rarely Seen:
Exorcism

The text of this service is Luke 8:22-39. It is the story of Jesus and the Gerasene demoniac. We invited the public servants of our city to attend this service as our guests. Letters went out weeks in advance. We encouraged our people to invite police officers, social workers, AA leaders, hospital emergency room personnel—anyone whose work placed them face-to-face with evil in its most blatant and violent forms.

Entrance

Opening songs focused on the power of God. In our contemporary service, we sang "Jesus, Mighty God," "A Mighty Fortress Is Our God," and "Praise the Name of Jesus." In our traditional service we sang "Come, Thou Almighty King," "A Mighty Fortress Is Our God," and "Crown Him King of Kings." We spoke words of welcome to our guests and offered a prayer on behalf of those who deal with the darkest side of life in our community.

Bad News

We watched a five-minute video clip from the movie *Grand Canyon.* (Note: if you use video clips, it is imperative that you own the license permitting such use or that you get permission from the producers of the film.) In this clip a man's car has broken down late at night in the inner city. He calls a tow truck whose driver arrives at the same time a gang begins to harass him. The tow truck operator and the gang leader have a discussion about their roles. The gang wants to be unhindered in robbing the driver. The tow truck operator wants the gang to leave and let him do his job. The gang leader has a gun and asserts that respect is gained only at the point of a gun. The operator of the tow truck speaks the pivotal line in the scene—"Man, it's not supposed to be this way." The congregation has seen a picture of a dark, threatening world.

The preacher walks to the pulpit, opens the local Sunday morning paper, and reads the dark news headlines from the community—shootings, robberies, crowded jails, child abuse. The Bad News laps over into the beginning of the sermon as the preacher continues:

When I read these kinds of things, it makes me want to run and hide. But that raises the question, "Who will face this evil?" I find myself thinking about

- a police officer that knocks on the door of domestic violence
- the social worker that sits across the table from a child abuser
- a teacher face-to-face with an angry student
- an emergency room team treating opposing gang members

- a public defender in a cold courtroom
- an undercover drug agent making a bust
- the counselor of a client who has purchased a gun
- a prison guard breaking up a fight with no one watching his back

These people can't run. It's their job. They face evil daily in its rawest, deadliest forms.

Good News

Have you ever wondered what Jesus might mean to these public servants? Listen to this story from the Gospel of Luke.

(Preacher reads Luke 8:22-39.)

The geography of the story is simple. The lake is in the middle. On one side of the lake is the safe, religious world of the Jews—the comfort zone. On the other side of the lake is the wild, threatening land of the Gentiles—the chaos zone. The sea, the mythical home of the devil in the deep blue sea, separates these two turfs.

En route from one side to the other, the devil brews a storm that scares seasoned sailors spitless. Sheer fear seizes them. They wake Jesus. Jesus rebukes the storm. *Rebuke* is an interesting word to use for storm-stilling. It's the same word Luke usually uses for demon-busting. Jesus speaks. The storm stops.

This reminds me of my eighth grade shop teacher, Mr. Craft. Don't you think that's a good name for a shop teacher? Mr. Craft. He'd walk in on 30 eighth graders horsing around with hammers, boards, and power tools. He'd say one word: "Boys!" And you could hear a pin drop.

I wonder what Jesus said to the storm? "Boys!" Or maybe just, "Shhh!" The disciples were now as awed by Jesus as they were by the storm. "Who is this?" They were beginning to catch on that the Most High God had put on skin and crawled into their boat. But before they had time to figure it out, they arrived on the other side.

It was Gentile territory, gang turf, the devil's ground. And a man in whom the devil had brewed a mess immediately greeted them. Townspeople had incarcerated him in chains, but he broke loose. He used to live in a house with his family. Now he lived in a graveyard, the abode of the unclean bodies and spooks. He was wild, naked, uncontrollable, nasty, loud, threatening. He was chock-full of demons. Demons had separated him from his family, his home, his town, his friends, his clothes, his sanity, his senses. And now demons had taken over his voice and were talking to Jesus through him.

The Exorcist was recently rereleased. A poll on *Good Morning America* says that it is still the scariest movie of all time. Something inside tells us that nothing is as frightening as what the devil can do given free reign inside a human body. The demons see Jesus and want to know their fate. They suddenly become like eighth grade boys in Mr. Craft's shop class. Jesus asks their name. They are Legion, which means 5,600. We've met most of them. They have names: Rage, Anger, Envy, Violence, Prejudice, Abuse, Rape, Drugs, Alcohol, Wildness, Pornography, Murder, Theft, Madness. They have names, and they do great harm.

This man is their poster child. He is their apartment complex. He is their post office box.

I don't know about you, but if I'm one of the disciples, I'm backtracking toward the boat.

I love Luke's comic relief. The demons know they are about to be evicted, and they beg to go live in a nearby herd of pigs. They prefer the low-rent district of squealing, mud-wallowing pigs to "the abyss." Jesus lets them move into the pigs. Once there they make a beeline to the sea, the residence of the devil in the deep blue sea. They are going home to papa. But little do they know that Jesus just put papa in his place on the way over.

Then we meet the townspeople. They never really cared about the guy. They just wanted him out of their hair. Chained or out in the cemetery, it didn't matter, as long as they didn't have to deal with him. It seems that government, at best, can only restrain and relocate evil. There are limits to our human efforts to corral evil. When the townspeople hear about the man and the pigs, they go out to see what's going on. The change is awesome. The wild man sits at Jesus' feet. The naked man is wearing clothes. The demented man is in his right mind. The destructive man is at peace. The chained man is calm. And the townspeople say the same thing to Jesus that the demons said, "Please go away. Please leave us alone. We are managing fine as we are." They are more afraid of Jesus than they are of the wild man.

Had I been these townspeople, I hope I'd have said,

- "Jesus, would You come to our jail. There are some people I want You to meet."
- "Jesus, would You mind spending a day at the Department of Child and Family Services? There are some angry men I'd like You to meet."
- "Jesus, would You meet with a senior high student who keeps threatening to beat me up if I fail him?"
- "Jesus, would You come with me on a drug bust?"

Do you know what I think? I think Jesus would have said, "Yes, yes, yes, yes." He goes with us into the storm of evil that threatens to sink our community. He goes with us to deal with hostile, angry, hateful demons that have taken up residence inside our fellow humans. He goes with us to jails, courtrooms, crime scenes, emergency rooms, dark alleys, angry homes, drug busts, and drunken brawls. He goes with us to the end of the earth. It's where He's always been going. And if we dare read ahead in Luke 9:1-2, we discover that it's where Jesus is sending us.

Response of the People

Can Jesus really go with us to these places? Hear the testimony of Lt. Matt Adamson, area director of our drug enforcement team. (*Enter Matt.*)

Matt gave a powerful testimony of God's call to service and guidance in his career. We invited all the public servants to stand. We thanked them for their work and asked the people seated around them to surround them for a moment of prayer. We prayed for them. In one service the choir sang "Heal Our Land." In our other service a soloist sang "We Can Make a Difference."

Blessing

May the power of God send you from this sanctuary to the darkest corners of our city. May you find courage to face the evil that threatens you and your neighbor. May you see demons flee from the people being set free in Christ. May the Spirit of loving power rest on you in fullness.

WEEK THREE
Holy Habits Rarely Seen:
Tending the Right Gap

For this service, you will see the work sheet developed eight weeks in advance. The sermon text and guiding idea is sketched but undeveloped. The text is the story of the Pharisee and tax collector in Luke 18:9-14. They pray radically different prayers and receive surprising responses from God. The central idea is how we measure ourselves spiritually. Our worship team created this work sheet to guide the plot of the service.

Entrance

The standard to which we should aspire is Christlikeness. Opening songs, scriptures, prayer, and welcome will focus on the desire to be made like God.

Bad News

Our drama team will develop a humorous look at Pharisaical measuring sticks in a modern-day church. A pastor will line his people up for inspection and compare them with each other. (Linda Stone wrote a hilarious drama titled "The Review" in which a character named Pastor Howitzer inspects the troops.) We have discovered that humor works best when it comes to revealing things about ourselves we don't easily admit.

Good News

Two men stand to pray in the Temple. They live radically different lifestyles. The Pharisee was every bit as good as he said he was in his prayer. And the tax collector was every bit as evil as the Pharisee said he was. But the tax collector goes home justified. Why? Because the Pharisee recognized the gap between himself and the tax collector and offered the difference to God. The tax collector recognized the gap between himself and God and asked for mercy.

Response of the People

We will offer people a time of prayer. We will ask them to offer their prayer to God. They may either tell God how much better they are than other people they know, or they may recognize the gap between themselves and God. If they choose the latter, we suggest they pray the prayer of the tax collector: "God, be merciful to me, a sinner!" (v. 13). Closing music will celebrate the mercy of God to forgive.

Blessing

Send the people into the world measuring themselves by looking into the face of Jesus, the perfect mirror of humanity.

(Note: The two dramas referenced in this section, and

other original productions, are available from Linda Stone. You can contact her at www.lstone@college church.org.)

B.

The Creation of a Worshiping People
(Or Exodus Exegeted in 11 Pages)

Note: People often underestimate the importance of worship to God. This chapter is a sermon about worship. Enjoy.

"Good morning, Mr. Moses. Your mission, should you decide to accept it, is to go down into Egypt and tell Pharaoh to let My people go. I have heard their cries and am sending you to bring them out of slavery. Your goal on this mission is to bring them back to this same spot and to worship Me on this very mountain. I will be with you. This tape will self-destruct in 30 seconds."

And so begins the story of the creation of a worshiping people. God our Creator is best understood from the future. God is calling into existence that which does not yet exist. Like a parent beckoning an infant to take his or her first step, God is in our future calling us into existence as His holy people. The greatest work of creation is the resurrection of Jesus. God stood on the future side of the grave and called Jesus to life. It is the model for everything that is being brought to completion by the Creator God. The story of Exodus is our story. It is the Old Testament equivalent of the Resurrection.

The story begins with

- A barefoot man standing before a burning bush
- A people crying out in oppression
- A God who hears cries, sets free, and calls for worship as the grateful response of liberation

Moses offered token excuses to the mission, but God countered every excuse. And before we know it, Moses and his smooth-talking PR pal, Aaron, are standing in front of Pharaoh making their speeches.

> But Pharaoh said, "Who is the LORD, that I should heed him and let Israel go? I do not know the LORD, and I will not Israel go." Then they said, "The God of the Hebrews has revealed himself to us; let us go a three days' journey into the wilderness to sacrifice to the LORD our God, or he will fall upon us with a pestilence or sword." But the king of Egypt said to them, "Moses and Aaron, why are you taking the people away from their work? Get to your labors!" (Exod. 5:2-4).

It appears that this may well be "mission impossible." Pharaoh decides that if they have time to think about unionizing, they apparently aren't working hard enough.

So he increases the daily brick quota at the Goshen factory. He makes their life harder than ever.

The pressures of work are a challenge to the worshiping people of God. We are easily consumed by the demand to produce. Pharaoh is still raising the brick quota and calling for more. It's hard to fit worship into a world driven by Pharaoh.

Where we would tend to cave in to Pharaoh's demands and make more bricks, God steps up to the challenge with a round of plagues. The dialogue between God and Pharaoh begins to sound like a broken record.

GOD: Let My people go so they may worship Me.

PHARAOH: No.

GOD: Plague No. 1: water turned to blood

GOD: Let My people go so they may worship Me.

PHARAOH: No.

GOD: Plague No. 2: heaps of frogs

GOD: Let My people go so they may worship Me.

PHARAOH: No.

GOD: Plague No. 3: gnats galore

GOD: Let My people go so they may worship Me.

PHARAOH: No.

GOD: Plague No. 4: swarms of flies

I think you get the point. Each time, the command to let the people go is based on their need to worship God. The next three dialogues bring on plagues 5, 6, and 7, that is, sick livestock, boils, and hail. Under threat of locusts, some of Pharoah's officials suggest that he rethink his position.

Pharaoh's officials said to him, "How long shall this fellow be a snare to us? Let the people go, so that they may worship the LORD their God; do you not yet understand that Egypt is ruined?" So Moses and Aaron were brought back to Pharaoh, and he said to them, "Go, worship the LORD your God! But which ones are to go?" Moses said, "We will go with our young and our old; we will go with our sons and daughters and with our flocks and herds, because we have the LORD's festival to celebrate." He said to them, "The LORD indeed will be with you, if ever I let your little ones go with you! Plainly, you have some evil purpose in mind. No, never! Your men may go and worship the LORD, for that is what you are asking." And they were driven out from Pharaoh's presence *(10:7-11)*.

Pharaoh is no dummy. Three days away from the family would make the men of Israel as homesick as a group of Promise Keepers. But Moses refuses the offer. Either we all go worship, or none of us goes. Apparently it matters to God that the generation gap be bridged in worship. It is for young and old, Grandpa and little Freddie. Families do this together.

Pharaoh stiffens again. Plague No. 8 follows—loads of locusts. Plague No. 9 is next—darkness where Pharaoh lived but broad daylight in the Israelite camp. Pharaoh decides it's time to talk again.

Then Pharaoh summoned Moses, and said, "Go, worship the LORD. Only your flocks and your herds shall remain behind. Even your children may go with you." But Moses said, "You must also let us have sacrifices and burnt offerings to sacrifice to the LORD our God. Our livestock also must go with us; not a hoof shall be left behind, for we must choose some of them for the worship of the LORD our God, and we will not know what to use to worship the LORD until we arrive there." But the LORD hardened Pharaoh's heart, and he was unwilling to let them go. Then Pharaoh said to him, "Get away from me! Take care that you do not see my face again, for on the day you see my face you shall die." Moses said, "Just as you say! I will never see your face again" *(vv. 24-29).*

The conversation has turned deadly. Pharaoh suggests they go worship without their livestock—their money. Moses refuses. When the people of God appear for worship, everything is made available to God. When we worship, we bring everything we have before God. He has total rights to our cows and our cash. We leave nothing behind. Pharaoh just doesn't get it. But he is about to.

Plague No. 10 brings death. In every home in Egypt,

someone is dead. God has brought the strongest nation in the world to its knees for one reason—so that His people may worship Him. God is serious about our worship.

Exodus 12 is the account of the Passover meal. God's people are given instructions on how to avoid a visit from the death angel. A supper is instituted. The supper calls for sacrificial blood, traveling clothes, and a costly deliverance. The shadow of this historic meal falls across every Communion table. God's people are going on a journey toward freedom, and worship is the ultimate destiny. They leave behind a nation in shambles and begin their journey to the holy mountain. Along the way, they reveal that they have much to learn. God provides and teaches. And finally, they arrive at burning-bush mountain, Mount Sinai. Moses has accomplished the mission. He is home—almost.

In Exod. 20, God calls Moses up on the mountain and gives him instructions for the people. It should be no surprise that heading the list is the command to worship the Lord and no one else. The lawgiving goes on for four whole chapters. God doesn't miss anything. His law defines community life, justice, care for the needy, retaliation for violence, sexual relationships, crop rotation, Sabbath rest, and annual worship festivals. His liberated people are to live like their Liberator. "I, the Lord your God am holy; be holy in all you do" (author's paraphrase). We are set free for freedom. At the core of our worship is the reminder that we are called to be holy.

Moses faithfully delivers God's law to the people.

They agree to live by it. All is well. They enter into a blood covenant. Each now has the right to expect certain behavior of the other in light of promises made. They are oath-bound, blood-sealed, law-loving covenant partners.

Following the covenant ratification ceremony, Moses goes back up on the mountain. He is there for 40 days and nights. What did God and Moses talk about all that time? Read Exod. 25—31 and you'll see. For seven long chapters, God tells Moses how worship is to be done. In Genesis, it takes all of 31 verses to tell the story of the creation of the world. Here, it takes 243 verses for God to tell Moses how the people are to worship.

They talk about a Tent of Meeting, also known as a Tabernacle. It is to be placed in the center of the camp as a way of reminding the people that worship lies at the center of life. It isn't something on the periphery of a busy community. It's the hub of all we do. God talks about dimensions, colors, layout, altar, tables, basins, lampstands, the ark of the covenant, the seat of mercy, the bread of the presence, the oil of anointing, and the garb of the priest. Do you get the feeling that our worship matters to God? The places we gather are holy because God is among us. We are moved in these places by what we see and hear and smell and touch and taste. Those who lead us in worship should be prepared. Exodus 25—31 is rarely studied in depth. The details overwhelm us. But buried in the details are rich truths about our worship.

Meanwhile, back at the ranch, the Israelites are getting restless. Moses' fickle associate pastor, Aaron, has gotten itchy trying to explain Moses' 40-day disappearing act. The people decide to pass the plates, collect gold, and fashion a golden calf in honor of the God who brought us up out of Egypt (see Exod. 32). They have a big party for the calf. How do they know to do this? Apparently, people instinctively worship. They just aren't sure what or who to worship. Without God and godly leaders, people will find something to devote their lives to. Watch sports enthusiasts. Watch Wall Street investors. Watch doting grandparents. We will find something to worship, something to give our gold to, something to dance around. God's response is swift:

> The LORD said to Moses, "Go down at once! Your people, whom you brought up out of the land of Egypt, have acted perversely; they have been quick to turn aside from the way that I commanded them; they have cast for themselves an image of a calf, and have worshiped it and sacrificed to it, and said, 'These are your gods, O Israel, who brought you up out of the land of Egypt!'" The LORD said to Moses, "I have seen this people, how stiff-necked they are. Now let me alone, so that my wrath may burn hot against them and I may consume them; and of you I will make a great nation" *(32:7-10)*.

I feel sorry for Moses. When he stood at the burning

bush, he heard God say, "I have heard the cries of *My* people" (see Exod. 3). Now God says to Moses, *"Your* people . . . have acted perversely"* (32:7, emphasis added). God no longer identifies with this calf-worshiping, covenant-breaking people. He is ready to wipe them out and start all over again with Moses and create for himself a people who will worship Him. And don't think God can't do it. He started with an old childless couple named Abraham and Sarah when He created Israel. God can do it again.

After all God has done to liberate these people, He is ready to destroy them for one reason—they worship other gods. Moses intervenes with an appeal to God's honor and name. "What will the Egyptians think? That You lured these people out here in the wilderness to destroy them? What kind of a God will they believe You are?" God relented (see vv. 11-14). Apparently it matters to God how others interpret His relationship with His people. God lets them live. But that's not the end of the story.

In Exod. 32, the sons of Levi are inducted into the priesthood by the bloody act of slaying calf-worshipers. Moses says to them at the end of the killing, "Today you have ordained yourselves for the service of the LORD, each one at the cost of a son or a brother, and so have brought a blessing on yourselves this day" (v. 29). The leaders of worship must care more about what God wants than what the people want. Sometimes the role of a priest is bloody.

In light of this worship disaster, the journey seems to be in jeopardy. Will God go with these people to the Promised Land? Moses and God discuss the matter.

[God] said, "My presence will go with you [singular], and I will give you [singular] rest." And [Moses replied], "If your presence will not go, do not carry us [plural] up from here. For how shall it be known that I have found favor in your sight, I and your people, unless you go with us? In this way, we shall be distinct, I and your people, from every people on the face of the earth" *(33:14-16)*.

The primary issue for Moses is the presence of God. The only thing that distinguishes us as the people of God is His presence in our worship. An absent God calls into question our reason for gathering. God again relents and commits to keep covenant with these people. But He issues a stern warning about worshiping the pagan gods they will encounter along the way.

Before they set out, God calls Moses back up on the mountain one last time. This time, when he returns to camp, his face is shining. He begins to teach the people. We find his sermon in chapters 35—40. It's a long speech. And guess what it's about? You guessed it. Worship. He tells them how to build the tent of meeting. He gives them its dimensions, colors, and layout. He names the subcontractors. He tells them to put it in the center of the camp. He calls for altars, basins, lampstands, an ark of the covenant, a seat of mercy, the bread of the presence, and oil of anointing. He instructs them in priestly dress, sacrifice, and offerings. At the end of his speech the story comes to an end with these words:

> Then the cloud covered the tent of meeting, and the glory of the LORD filled the tabernacle. Moses was not able to enter the tent of meeting because the cloud settled upon it, and the glory of the LORD filled the tabernacle. Whenever the cloud was taken up from the tabernacle, the Israelites would set out on each stage of their journey; but if the cloud was not taken up, then they did not set out until the day that it was taken up. For the cloud of the LORD was on the tabernacle by day, and fire was in the cloud by night, before the eyes of all the house of Israel at each stage of their journey *(40:34-38).*

Worship characterizes the journey of the people of God, from the moment of our liberation from slavery to our arrival in the Promised Land, and every day along the way. God has created a worshiping people. All praise be to God.

C.

Invitation to the Dance
(A Theology of Worship)

One of the great worship hymns of our times finds us singing, "God in three Persons, blessed Trinity." If God is to be understood like we understand "persons," what does this say about our worship of God?

Our culture identifies a person as
a separate individual
with an identifiable body,
a recognizable face,
and distinguishing characteristics.

In other words, we identify ourselves as separate skin-sacks of blood and bones.

If God is three persons, can we do with God what we can do with three persons? Can we separate God? Put Father in one room, Jesus in another, and the Spirit somewhere else? Can we get them to disagree? Can one vote

Democrat, one Republican, and one Independent? Can they divorce? Can we find characteristics true of one but not true of the other two?

Sure, these are silly questions. But maybe not as silly as some of our folk theology about God. Have you heard the one about the Father sitting miffed in heaven, ticked off with what we've done to His creation, and poor Jesus running around on earth trying to placate the Father so He'd love us again? Or the one about getting Jesus when I was saved but getting the Holy Spirit when I was sanctified? (Maybe this suggests a third work of grace in which we receive the Father!)

If we think of God as we think of persons, we can think silly things. But maybe our definition of *person* is all wrong. In the Bible a person is identified not by a separateness from others but by a connection to others. An Israelite is a son or daughter of Abraham. Saul is named as one who belongs to the tribe of Benjamin. Covenants unite people and give them their identity. Personhood is not our radical difference from each other but our radical belonging to each other.

And where did we learn this? By looking into the face of God. God cannot be divided into three pieces that make sense alone. When we say "God," we mean Father, Son, and Spirit. It is impossible to explain what any one of the three does without reference to the other two. God is inseparable. We would not know God as Father apart from Jesus revealing this to us. God is rarely spoken of as "Father" in the Old Testament. It is Jesus who teaches us to pray "Our Father." The Spirit is the breath of God who creates and resurrects. Into the dark, formless chaos God breathes. Into the dead body of Jesus, God breathes. We call this the Holy Spirit. Jesus as Risen Lord is incomprehensible apart from the Holy Breath of God, the Spirit. The Father who creates sends the Son who redeems through the Spirit who sanctifies us into the union that exists as Father, Son, and Spirit.

Have you ever seen three children in a circle, holding hands, going round and round in an ecstasy of laughter, love, rhythm, and unity? This is a picture of the Trinity. That there are three means a decision has been made to be inclusive. Movement depends on paying attention to the others. Each follows in step. No one leads. The joy on each face is a reflection of the joy on the other two. Life and energy exist in the center of the circle.

This idea of God as a circle dance is not original. It is very old. *Perichoresis* is the technical term for circle dance. And I think we can learn some things about worship from this image of God.

Worship is possible because it is already going on in the center of this circle. The idea that worship occurs when we come together to execute (pun intended) a worship service is misinformed. Worship does not begin with our Entrance. Worship has been going on forever among

Father, Son, and Spirit. The Entrance simply reminds us that we are graciously invited into the fellowship known as Trinity. God has extended the invitation in the name of Jesus. We step into a stream of worship that started before the world was formed. We are latecomers. And lest we think that a contemporary worship movement has discovered something new, we need to remember that creativity in worship is the gift that flows from the center of this circle dance.

One Wednesday night, we divided our congregation into three groups and sang in a round. We were singing "Father, I Adore You," with separate lines for Jesus and the Holy Spirit.

Our sanctuary extends in three directions, all facing the center pulpit. As people sang, they were actually looking at each other. It was a beautiful moment as different words rose and fell in the mixture of sounds. We were singing three different lines at one time, but one song. It was godly. This was not something we created. We were being drawn into the circle dance of God, where Father, Son, and Spirit move in perfect rhythm singing to each other the song of self-emptying adoration. Imagine it. The Father sings His adoration to Jesus, and Jesus sings at the same time His adoration back to the Father.

Jesus is offering himself to God as a sacrifice for our sins. He is offering His perfect obedience on our behalf. And both Father and Son sing love to the Spirit who proceeds from them to create and resurrect the world and its creatures.

God is singing an eternal round of love, adoration, life, and self-emptying grace. And we are invited into this circle.

Worship is not something we do for God. It is the gift of God to people who have no invitation to the dance of life. We were sitting at home, dead, without a lover, and the-Father-in-Christ-through-the-Spirit invited us into a circle of holy love. We experience rhythm and love and unity that we didn't create. The fact that we can worship is sheer grace. Worship is the ongoing reality of the Trinity in which we are called to participate.

Our Week and Our Worship

This view of God as a circle dance also suggests that our worship is not dependent on the kind of week we've had.

Have you ever found yourself thinking that God can't wait to see you on Sunday to congratulate you for your sainthood over the previous six days? You had personal devotions every day. You led someone to Jesus. You paid your tithe and gave beyond. You said the right words and did the right deeds. You came to church believing you had done something that would put a smile on God's face. Today you can really worship! You have something to offer!

On the flip side, you had a horrid week. No devotions. You didn't crack your Bible one time. The tithe money is at the dentist's office. The last straw broke on Thursday afternoon and you told your boss what you really think. You were an absolute grouch at home. The neighbors probably heard you explaining reality to your 15-year-old son. You wake up on Sunday morning and the last place you want to be is church. You have nothing to offer God. You have disappointed Him all week long. He doesn't want to see you. You're not going.

Do you ever find yourself thinking like this? Good week = I can worship. Bad week = I can't show up. There is a phrase for this kind of thinking. It's called having "confidence in the flesh" (Phil. 3:3). It is believing that our worship is acceptable or unacceptable based on what we've done or not done. And this is wrong.

Our worship is acceptable through the mediation of Jesus, our High Priest. We place too much emphasis on ourselves when we think of worship as dependent on our doings. Worship is about the God who dances in a circle of grace. We can come just as we are, good week or bad. What makes us acceptable is not what we have to offer but what Jesus offers on our behalf.

Does this suggest it doesn't matter how we live? That we can worship on Sunday and go live like the devil all week long? That we leave worship and collect sin like a garbage truck, only to dump it on God again next Sunday? No, it doesn't mean that at all. It means our lives become acts of worship, offered to the Father, in the name of Jesus, empowered through the Spirit.

I appeal to you therefore, brothers and sisters, by the mercies of God, to present your bodies as a living sacrifice, holy and acceptable to God, which is your spiritual worship. Do not be conformed to this world, but be transformed by the renewing of your minds, so that you may discern what is the will of God— what is good and acceptable and perfect *(Rom. 12:1-2).*

Our lives are the outflow of being graced in the circle dance. We are a reflection of what we have experienced from God.

How We Think About Congregation

What does it mean to be a person who is part of a worshiping congregation?

Our cultural definition of *person* would be

- I am an individual.
- I am distinguishable from you.
- I have a Social Security number that is different from yours.
- I exist in this identifiable skin-sack.
- I make choices in line with my ruling desires.
- I enter relationships that are meaningful to me.
- I seek out experiences that are relevant to me.
- I have limited time and do not want to waste it on uninteresting people.
- I am not obligated to you unless I choose to be, and

you have no right to expect anything from me unless I give you that right.

- I am responsible for myself.

This is the dominant theology of our culture regarding humans. There is a good label for this person. Call him or her a *consumer.* This individual is reaching out into the world, taking things into himself or herself. This person consumes experiences, people, and things.

By stark contrast, the biblical definition of *person* would be

- I am a child of God.
- I belong to the people of God by baptism.
- I exist as a body in a body.
- I take interest in the lives of my brothers and sisters.
- I seek to be faithful to them.
- I am in relationships that are given. Some are energizing; some are draining.
- I am obligated. People have the right to expect certain things of me in light of the covenant that exists between us.
- I cannot think of myself apart from the Body of Christ.
- I am a new creation.

This is the dominant theology of Scripture regarding humans. There is a good label for this person. Call him or her a *member.* This individual belongs to all who are in Christ and views the world through this lens.

When you think "member," think biologically, such as a family member or a member of the human body—an arm, a leg, a neck. We find that word in the Bible:

For as in one body we have many *members*, and not all the *members* have the same function, so we, who are many, are one body in Christ, and individually we are *members* one of another *(Rom. 12:4-5, emphasis added).*

So then you are no longer strangers and aliens, but you are citizens with the saints and also *members* of the household of God, built upon the foundation of the apostles and prophets, with Christ Jesus himself as the cornerstone. In him the whole structure is joined together and grows into a holy temple in the Lord; in whom you also are built together spiritually into a dwelling place for God *(Eph. 2:19-22, emphasis added).*

So then, putting away falsehood, let all of us speak the truth to our neighbors, for we are *members* of one another *(4:25, emphasis added).*

Being a member of the Body of Christ shapes our involvement with each other. We gather for worship at the invitation of God because this is what defines us. This is who we are. This is the place we recall our given identity. This is our family. These are our brothers and sisters. We are faithful to the gatherings, not to earn points with God but because this is essential to our very being.

This is why we attend

- When the preaching is boring
- When we don't know the babies being dedicated
- When it is rumored that the visiting missionary has slides
- When the guy who is leading music moves around too much
- When the songs are all out of the hymnal and slow

We attend because we are members, not consumers. Consumers check out the product and determine whether or not they wish to consume it. Members just show up because they belong.

This places new weight on the meaning and practice of baptism into the Body of Jesus. In baptism, we are giving people a new identity. We now have the right to expect things of them. We are bound to them and they to us in ways we cannot ignore without damage to the Body.

This places new weight on the meaning and practice of Communion. We are at the table together. Communion is not an intimate dinner for two—just Jesus and me; just Jesus and you. It is the meal that was cooked up in the middle of a circle dance. The aroma is compelling. We don't get our food and go eat under a tree. We sit down at the table with everyone else and share in the fellowship created by Father, Son, and Spirit. We look each other in the face and remember that we belong to each other in Christ. The Spirit is at work in the meal sanctifying us together as one.

This places new weight on infant baptism and dedication. This is not an "ooh and aah" moment for parents to show off their offspring. This is a covenant ceremony in which we lay claim to a human being and make promises to that family. I tell parents that if they aren't planning to raise this child in the church, they ought not do this. I tell them they are saying that they intend for this child to belong to us.

This places new weight on church membership. We ought to make it more meaningful than a name in a book. It is a person's decision to be identified with the visible people of God. They are joining the family as responsible servants and workers. They have the right to expect things of us, and we of them. We're asking far more than agreement with doctrine and ethics. We're asking them to understand that we actually belong to each other.

This places new weight on our worship gatherings. We are not consumers looking for a praise and worship pick-me-up. We are the Body of Christ, gathered in His name, participating as one in a circle dance of loving grace.

A RECOMMENDATION

Meaningful worship is no accident. God has given gifts for the preparation and planning of worship. Pastor and worship leaders could read and discuss this book together and design the planning process for worship. A worship team could be formed and a retreat planned for a discussion of *The Worship Plot*. Each member would then understand the plot of worship and know how his or her contribution fits into the whole.

Beyond this, the congregation could be invited to study *The Worship Plot* in Sunday School and small-group settings. Pastors could teach the five acts of worship in a midweek setting or new member's class. Newcomers could learn the congregational approach to worship.

When we know why we do what we do, we are better prepared to offer our worship to God. May God bless you as you seek to get all your people on the same page and in the same plot.